Joy in Church Membership

JOY IN
CHURCH MEMBERSHIP

DONALD F. ACKLAND

2271

Convention Press

Nashville, Tennessee

© 1955 · CONVENTION PRESS

NASHVILLE, TENNESSEE

Printed in the United States of America

100.MY 55 R.R.D.

About the Author

IN THE SPRING OF 1948, Donald F. Ackland, accompanied by his wife and three children, arrived in New York from England. Their destination was the South, where opportunities for Christian service beckoned.

For many years, the name of Donald F. Ackland had been familiar in Great Britain on Sunday school lesson helps, evangelistic tracts, and similar materials. He had entered Christian journalism immediately after graduation. Following six years as assistant editor of the weekly religious publication, *The Christian,* he went to the London City Mission to serve it for the next eighteen years in promotional and editorial capacities. During the war, he acted as the mission's secretary for war relief, sharing the common deprivations and dangers of the people of London, and seeking to help families stricken by the bombing.

Upon arrival in this country, because of his Baptist background and convictions, Donald Ackland soon became linked in service with Southern Baptists. In 1949, he joined the editorial staff of the Sunday School Board, and is now editor of *Open Windows, The Braille Baptist,* and general tracts. During the years he has lived in Nashville he has served several churches as interim pastor and is in demand throughout the South as preacher and teacher. He received his United States citizenship in 1953.

Contents

CHAPTER 1

Joy for You

ORDINARILY this would be called the Introduction. But somehow people skip introductions, and this is too important to be skipped. So it is being called chapter 1, for it is here that our study begins.

I. ARE YOU A CHRISTIAN?

1. *Life's Biggest Question*

In any setting or circumstance, the question, Are you a Christian? is of primary importance. It should be possible to answer it with a direct yes or no. Yet, strangely enough, when this question is addressed to most people, it is met at best with hesitation and at worst with indignation.

Ask a man whether he is an American and he will come straight back with his answer. Ask him whether he is a Christian and he will reply, "I hope so" or "I am trying to be." He may even snap back with something which sounds suspiciously like "Mind your own business." That this question is in a different category from others is evident from the way people react to it.

According to the Bible, there is no question more important for you to face. Upon your answer hang tremendous issues—of salvation and condemnation, of life and death, of heaven and hell. This question is important even for our present study, for this book is addressed to Christians and its contents can be of value only to those who return a firm, positive answer to the inquiry, Are you a Christian?

2. *A Christian Defined*

There is no need for uncertainty in answering this question. Neither is there any element of foolish pride or of unwarranted confidence in being able to say, "Yes, I am a Christian." For the Christian is one who can declare with the apostle Paul: "I have been crucified with Christ; and it is no longer I that live, but Christ liveth in me: and that life which I now live in the flesh I live in faith, the faith which is in the Son of God, who loved me, and gave himself up for me" (Gal. 2:20 ASV). To be a Christian is to link one's life with Jesus by faith in his death for our sins and by fellowship with him in the power of his resurrection. It furnishes no reason for conceit or self-commendation, but only for gratitude to him whose name we bear. For a Christian is *Christ's* man.

3. *Tests to Apply*

By these tests, then, are you a Christian? Have you realized your danger as a sinner? (Eph. 5:6). Have you seen in Jesus your only hope of pardon and of reconciliation with God? (Acts 4:12). Have you repented of your sin? (Acts 2:38). Have you come to him for the forgiveness which he dispenses at Calvary's cross? (Rom. 3:24). Have you accepted the assurance in your heart that God has received you as his child? (Gal. 4:4–7). Have you begun to walk in newness of life in the daily experience of his grace? (Rom. 6:4, 11).

If you are a Christian, here is a second question:

II. ARE YOU A CHURCH MEMBER?

1. *A Definition Stated*

What is meant by the word "church"? The question has often been asked and variously answered. We certainly do not use the word to indicate a building of any sort. Bricks and mortar do not constitute a church. Competent scholars agree that, in the majority of cases in which the word church (*ekklesia*) appears in the New Testament, it refers to a local congregation of believers (Acts 14:23, 27; Philemon 2; etc.). It is apparent that the word is applied to Christians in a more general sense in passages like Ephesians 1:22–23 and 5:27. This usage, however, cannot justify the description of a denomination as a church—an idea completely foreign to the New Testament. Throughout this book, the word church is used to indicate a group of baptized Christians banded together for worship, fellowship, and service.

2. *A Distinction Indicated*

It is important to distinguish between becoming a Christian and becoming a church member. The first should always lead to the second, but the two are not identical. To fail to see that conversion should be followed by membership in some particular church produces religious nomads—people who flit from meeting to meeting and make no true contribution to Christ's cause. On the other hand, church membership must never be made a substitute for a personal experience of salvation through faith in Christ. Many people may be entertaining the false confidence that all is well with them spiritually because they have submitted to certain rites and have their names on a church or parish roll.

3. *How We Become Church Members*

We become Christians by the activity of God. It is by the operation of his Holy Spirit that we are born again and receive the adoption of sons (John 1:12–13). But it is by our own decision and action, with the approval of other Christians, that our names are added to a church roll. The two things are distinct in the teaching of the New Testament and must be so kept in our thinking, if we are to avoid serious error. Of the early church it is said, "The Lord added to them day by day those that were saved" (Acts 2:47 ASV). They were saved first, and then they were added to the church.

4. *The Imperative of Church Membership*

It is both the duty and the privilege of every saved person to unite with a church. This was the divinely-appointed procedure from the beginning. When the gospel was first preached at Pentecost, men and women heard the saving message, were convicted of their sins, believed in the Lord Jesus Christ as their Saviour, confessed him publicly in baptism, and were received into the church (Acts 2:37–47). As the message spread, reaching centers like Antioch in Syria (Acts 11:19–26), new churches were formed as soon as converts were made. This also was the method of the apostle Paul. Wherever he went, and souls were brought out of paganism into the liberty of the gospel, there the believers were formed into churches for mutual fellowship and service.

The New Testament knows nothing of Christian experience practiced independently and in isolation from other Christians. Jesus began his public ministry by creating a circle of kindred souls, united in common love and loyalty to himself. He purposed that his followers should continue in this pattern. His promise of the power of the Holy Spirit became a glorious reality when the disciples were "with one accord in one place" (Acts 2:1). The same Holy Spirit, as the interpreter of the mind of Christ, makes our Christian duty clear. We are not to forsake "the assembling of ourselves together, as the manner of some is" (Heb. 10:25).

For the strengthening of our own experience, for our

continuing instruction in the Christian way, for the contribution that we can make to the faith of other believers,
for the privilege of fellowship in worship and witness, for
the more effective influence of a united testimony, for
obedience to the revealed will of Christ our Lord, it is
required of Christians that they be church members.

Supposing, therefore, that you are both a Christian and
a church member, permit this further question:

III. IS YOUR CHURCH MEMBERSHIP ALL YOU EXPECTED IT TO BE?

Perhaps it should be admitted that a great many people
enter upon church membership—as some do upon marriage—without a very clear idea as to what is involved. It
is to help remedy this condition that this book was written. There are certain standards by which we may judge
the satisfactions to be derived from being a member of a
church.

1. *Consider the First Believers*

For example, there is the standard of New Testament
experience. We cannot read the Acts or the epistles without recognizing that, to the early believers, being a Christian, with its parallel obligation of church membership,
was the greatest thing in their lives. Perhaps they did not
always do a very good job in their church membership,
but it was never a tame or an unimportant thing to them.

Those churches which were recipients of letters from
Paul and other apostles could not escape the thought that
they belonged to the most wonderful fellowship in the
world. Because they were united to Christ's church, it
was imperative that they guard their conduct, preserve
harmony among themselves, regard themselves as trustees
of God's truth, ever be active in their witness for Jesus
Christ, and be watchful for his coming again. Moreover,

they were expected to find joy in their church fellowship —joy which was independent of circumstances and which could triumph even over persecution (Phil. 4:4; 1 Peter 1:6–9).

2. *Christians of Our Acquaintance*

What, too, of the obvious happiness which some Christians of our acquaintance find in their church life? To look around any typical church is to find a nucleus of men and women, of boys and girls, of families to whom the church means more than can ever be put into words. The church's program is no chore to them, but a glorious opportunity for worship and witness to be eagerly accepted and fully used. They do not have to be persuaded to attend services and meetings; they can be depended upon to be present. They do not have to be coerced into accepting assignments; they are ever ready to take on responsibilities. They do not begrudge giving to the church budget; they tithe joyfully—and some give beyond their tithe. And all of this is done in a spirit of willing cheerfulness, without expectation of special recognition, as though to belong to the church and serve its interests were reward enough.

Such people are their pastor's "joy and crown," as Paul said of the Philippians. But they are also examples to others of what church membership should mean. They inspire the question:

IV. IS YOUR CHURCH MEMBERSHIP ALL IT OUGHT TO BE?

1. *Rewards of Loyalty*

While an active and loyal church membership brings rich satisfactions to the one who practices it, we are not primarily in the fellowship of the church for what we can get out of it but for what we can put into it. It happens to be one of the compensations of God's grace that those who do most for their church in supporting its program, sharing its ministries, and giving toward its needs derive the greatest blessings from their membership. But here, as in all other areas of Christian living, the Master's axiom holds good, "It is more blessed to give than to receive" (Acts 20:35).

2. *These Miss the Joy*

There are people who recognize their obligations in other spheres of life but who are careless in discharging their duty toward the church. They are irregular in attendance at its Sunday services. They are rarely if ever found in prayer meeting. They make erratic appearances at Sunday school and at Training Union. They give inadequately to the church's financial program, refusing to pledge, and complaining every time the preacher refers to the responsibilities of Christian stewardship. They resist all attempts to enlist them in active service, being adept at finding excuses for refusing assignments. Is it any wonder that they find little joy in belonging to their church?

Most members of civic clubs display a greater degree of loyalty toward those organizations than many Christians do toward their churches. We hear of men who have not missed attendance at their club's weekly meeting in twenty-five years. Wherever they travel they seek out the local organization and put in their attendance there. You would expect such men to wear their club emblem with pride, for the club means something to them—it is an important part of their lives.

3. *Invest Your Life*

Should Christians be less faithful to their church than

people are to social and secular organizations? Not only does gratitude to the Lord Jesus, as Head of the church (Eph. 5:23), demand that we take our membership seriously; not only does the privilege of belonging to "the body of Christ" (1 Cor. 12:27) require that we participate in its sacred functions; but also, if we are to experience those deep satisfactions which so glorious an association affords, we must be prepared to invest our lives in the church.

The Jewish worshiper, on his way up to the Temple to keep the feast, sang in anticipation, "Behold, how good and how pleasant it is for brethren to dwell together in unity! . . . there the Lord commanded the blessing, even life for evermore" (Psalm 133:1, 3). For Christian hearts, linked in fellowship and service within the church, there are joys which exceed the language of the psalmist and which belong to the richest, deepest, dearest, sweetest things of life.

SUGGESTED TOPICS FOR DISCUSSION

1. Discuss this statement: Being a church member is not the same thing as being a Christian.

2. Examine some of the excuses given against joining a church.

3. What examples are available to us of the joys of church membership? Invite examples from personal knowledge.

OUTLINE

CHAPTER 2

Joy in Qualifying

A GROUP OF twenty-four people, their right hands raised, stood before the judge in a United States district court. Slowly, deliberately, a phrase at a time, they repeated the oath of allegiance to this country. Then, in a few well-chosen words, the judge addressed the group. He reminded them that application and effort had been necessary to qualify for citizenship. This day's events were their reward. But the possession of citizenship, he said, would impose new responsibilities. These must be met in the same spirit of high purpose and endeavor.

Soon the ceremony was over and the court adjourned. Twenty-four smiling people received the warm congratulations of their friends to whom they proudly displayed their certificates of naturalization, all duly signed and sealed. It had not been an easy process for some of them. At least five years' residence in this country had first to be established. Proof of character was required, followed by study and examination in the American government and the Constitution. For part of the group, the elements of the English language had to be mastered. But these conditions had been accepted as both reasonable and right, and the effort required to comply had been cheerfully made. No wonder they were happy! They had sought a coveted privilege. They had fulfilled the immediate requirements. And, having qualified, they had received the highly-prized piece of paper which gave them, though foreign born, the rights and the privileges of native-born Americans.

All worth-while institutions and organizations have rules of membership and make continuing demand upon those who are honored by their membership. In centuries past, trade guilds challenged young men to become proficient in their skills that they might have the right to display the appropriate emblems outside their stores or workshops. Scientific and professional bodies still impose rigid conditions of knowledge and experience upon those who seek admittance to their fellowships. People who aspire to join lodges find that membership is granted only after exacting demands have been met. The cub scout who wants to become an eagle scout has to satisfy his leaders by passing various tests; and the young man who has ambitions to be an airplane pilot discovers that there is a heavy price to be paid first in study and endeavor.

Just as the value set on a diamond adds to the satisfaction of owning it, so these rules and regulations enhance the privilege of membership in the institutions concerned, and contribute to the pride and joy of successful aspirants. The boy who becomes a letter man in school athletics has had to work mighty hard to obtain this recognition, but that makes him additionally happy in receiving it. The man who wears a Phi Beta Kappa key may seem to give it undue prominence, but he surely has a right to for he had to sweat blood and tears to earn it.

Is there any membership of any kind which can compare with membership in the church? It will take the rest of this book to answer this question fully. But it is well to state our conclusion in advance and to say that church membership exceeds all others in importance, privilege, opportunity, and satisfaction. This satisfaction begins at the point of qualifying. There is no cheap and easy way into church membership. Because it offers a privilege unparalleled in this world, Christ-honoring church membership requires certain imperative qualifications.

What those qualifications are we shall find in the New Testament, which might be called the rule book of the church. In the New Testament we have the only authoritative information concerning the church—its character, its functions, its government, and its membership. In language of unmistakable clarity and insistence it tells us who are worthy church members and how they become worthy. We appeal to this book, then, for answer to our question, What are the qualifications for becoming a worthy church member?

I. SAVING FAITH

1. *The Practice of the Jerusalem Church*

To ascertain upon what terms people may be admitted to membership of a New Testament church we must go back to the first occasion upon which such admittance took place. This we find in Acts 2. On the day of Pentecost, after the coming of the Holy Spirit, Peter preached a great sermon to the assembled crowds. This sermon will well repay our study.

First, he explained the phenomenon of the gift of tongues by an appeal to the Old Testament. He reminded his hearers that the prophet Joel had foretold a mighty visitation of God's Spirit, which prophecy, he said, was being fulfilled before their eyes (14–21). Then he proceeded to claim that the Holy Spirit had been sent, in such marvelous manifestation of power, by none other than Jesus Christ, whom "ye have taken, and by wicked hands have crucified and slain." Setting a pattern for all apostolic preaching, he made the resurrection of Jesus his greatest argument, asserting that he had been raised from the dead by the power of God himself (22–32). Finally he proclaimed Jesus as Lord and Christ. Though they had crucified him, God had highly exalted him, in evidence of which he had bestowed his Spirit upon his people (33–36).

This Christ-centered preaching produced immediate results. "Men and brethren, what shall we do?" asked Peter's listeners. ("Repent, and be baptized,") was the answer, whereupon, we are told, "They that gladly received his word were baptized: and the same day there were added unto them about three thousand souls" (Acts 2: 41). But this was only the beginning of a great ingathering which brought a continuing accession of strength to the Jerusalem church. After verses which give us a glimpse of conditions within the fellowship of the church, we are told, "The Lord added to them day by day those that were saved [were being saved—*margin*]" (Acts 2:47 ASV).

Note that it is said of this growing fellowship that they "did eat their meat with gladness and singleness of heart, praising God, and having favour with all the people" (Acts 2:46–47). Evidently they were a happy group whose joy was infectious. They had reason for happiness on every count. The things which qualified them for church membership provided occasion for praise. Had they not been aroused to a recognition of their guilt in the sight of God and of their consequent danger of eternal judgment? Had they not also repented of their sin and received the forgiveness of God? They were like men who had been first condemned and then acquitted, and their joy knew no bounds.

2. *The Teaching of the Apostles*

Apostolic preaching and teaching, as recorded in the Acts and the epistles, recognized no qualification for church membership which did not begin with repentance for sin and faith in the Lord Jesus Christ as Saviour. Again and again, when writing to the churches, Paul exhorted believers to recall their salvation and its cost, and to be grateful. The happiness of church membership begins here, for nothing is more wonderful than to know that past sin has been forgiven by that love of God which did not stop short of Calvary to accomplish its purpose. "Being justified by faith, we have peace with God through our Lord Jesus Christ: by whom also we have access by faith into this grace wherein we stand, and rejoice in hope of the glory of God. . . . And not only so, but we also joy in God through our Lord Jesus Christ, by whom we have now received the atonement" (Rom. 5 : 1–2, 11). If we would go more often to the cross, we would be more radiant Christians.

3. *A Distinctive of Baptists*

Baptists, taking the New Testament as the sole rule and authority for church doctrine and practice, insist upon a personal experience of salvation, involving both repentance and faith, as an indispensable prerequisite for church membership. Whether the procedures of some churches in receiving new members have always reflected this conviction is open to question. Who can doubt that Peter fully satisfied himself, in company with the rest of the disciples, that those who professed faith in Christ on the day of Pentecost had genuinely experienced the saving and transforming grace of God? Until thus satisfied, would they have accepted them as members of the church? Today we can lay no claim to a full measure of apostolic discernment and should exercise every care in determining that those who seek the privilege of church membership possess the basic spiritual qualifications. Are the methods we follow in receiving new members adequate for this? This question is worthy of careful study on the part of every church.

This is certain: There can be no real joy in church membership unless the membership has been gained on a true profession of Christian experience. The Gibeonites deceived the Israelites into making a league with them (Josh. 9). When their falsehood was discovered, they were spared from punishment but were only permitted to remain in the camp as "hewers of wood and drawers of water." They were *with* Israel but not *of* Israel. Who could expect them to understand the privileges and taste the joys of God's people? So those who obtain church membership without meeting God's terms exclude themselves from those joys which belong to the redeemed, and to them alone.

II. WILLING OBEDIENCE

1. *The Master's Commission*

Before the Lord Jesus returned to his Father's house, he gave to his apostles, in the Great Commission, explicit instructions concerning their continuing task. "Go ye therefore, and teach all nations, baptizing them in the name of the Father, and of the Son, and of the Holy Ghost: teaching them to observe all things whatsoever I have commanded you" (Matt. 28:19–20). Thus baptism was made a matter of obedience both in the proclamation of the gospel and in the response of those who believed. The faithful preacher and teacher must include baptism in his presentation of the call of God to unregenerate men; and the convert to Christianity must submit to the ordinance as the Saviour's own requirement of him.

2. *New Testament Procedure*

The apostles clearly understood that baptism stood between conversion and church membership. At Pentecost, the first ingathering of believing people was marked by a great baptismal service, or possibly by a series of such services since three thousand candidates were immersed

(Acts 2:41). Philip, the deacon evangelist, who brought a revival to the city of Samaria through his preaching, evidently included baptism in his messages, for we are told of his converts that "when they believed . . . they were baptized" (Acts 8:12). The same man, when engaged in personal soul-winning, laid emphasis on the need for baptism on the part of new believers so that the Ethiopian eunuch himself asked the question, "See, here is water; what doth hinder me to be baptized?" (Acts 8:36). Saul, who became Paul, lost no time in going through the baptismal waters as evidence of his change of heart and acceptance of Christ as his Saviour (Acts 9:18). And Peter, God's specially selected messenger to Cornelius the Roman, having first gained the consent of the Christians present, gave command that the converts among the Gentiles should "be baptized in the name of the Lord" (Acts 10:48).

3. *The Significance of Baptism*

This line of study may profitably be pursued throughout the Acts, a course recommended to the student. Such a study would reveal that the invariable practice of the apostles, to whom Christ committed his gospel and the care of his churches, was to uphold baptism as essential to Christian obedience. Its rich symbolism held significance for the convert and for all of his circle of acquaintance. It marked a break with the past as real as though the candidate had died. It declared the beginning of a new life as with a person brought back from the grave. It identified the convert with Christ his Saviour in his death, burial, and resurrection. "We are buried with him by baptism into death: that like as Christ was raised up from the dead by the glory of the Father, even so we also should walk in newness of life" (Rom. 6:4).

The believer who enters the baptismal pool honors his

Lord by obeying and confessing him. This should bring
to him deep, spiritual joy. Love always finds its fullest
satisfaction in fulfilling the wishes of the beloved. Many
testify to the day of their baptism as being one of the
happiest days of their lives. For them the joy of forgiveness and salvation is followed by the joy of submission to
the Saviour's will and of testimony to his name.

4. *Is the Method Important?*

This matter of obedience, and of the joy which flows
from it, invites an answer to the question, Is it necessary
that the New Testament mode of baptism be followed?
If Christ our Lord has indicated a particular method, it
most certainly is necessary. If his apostles consistently
enjoined and practiced a particular method, it most certainly is necessary. And there is no disagreement among
reputable scholars, whatever their denominational background, that the invariable New Testament practice was
immersion. The symbolism breaks down if any other
method is substituted, for only a submerged body can
represent death, and we forfeit the picture of resurrection
unless the same body is raised again from its watery
grave.

James M. Shelburne gave an excellent illustration of
this point in his story of the person who declared that the
amount of water used in baptism was of small importance.
"We don't use much," he said of his denomination, "but
I guess it will do just as well." "Suppose you did not have
a picture of your mother," said Dr. Shelburne in reply,
"and suppose, too, it was difficult to get a picture of your
mother, and I should say that I have a picture of a very
beautiful elderly woman and shall be glad to give you
that. You would say, 'That's very kind of you, but what I
want is a picture of my mother.'" Continuing, he said,
"Baptism is a pictorial representation of two great facts

which need constant emphasis and deserve to be kept before the minds of men. These facts are the burial and resurrection of Jesus. The reason why I cannot agree that your baptism will do just as well is that it is not as good a picture of the facts for which baptism stands."

Obedience, then, must be implicit and complete; and, when we go all the way with our Master, who was himself immersed at the hands of John the Baptist, we have the reward of our obedience in the joy that fills our hearts.

III. RIGHT BELIEF

1. *Does It Matter What We Believe?*

There is an easy-going philosophy in the world today, as dangerous as it is prevalent, that it does not matter what a person believes so long as he believes something. An idea closely related to this, and equally erroneous, is that one religion is as good as another.

Such notions can find no support in the Bible. There religion is presented, not as a matter of human investigation and inquiry, but of divine revelation. "God, who at sundry times and in divers manners spake in time past unto the fathers by the prophets, hath in these last days spoken unto us by his Son" (Heb. 1:1–2). This being true, we cannot think of God speaking with more than one voice. Both Old and New Testaments tell us that "the word of the Lord endureth for ever" (Isa. 40:8; 1 Peter 1:25). To this, Peter added the significant statement, "And this is the word which by the gospel is preached unto you." God has only one word for men, written in the Scriptures and incarnate in his Son; and this word alone is to be believed.

That the final destiny of men is determined by what they believe is a solemn thought. "He that believeth on him [Jesus] is not condemned: but he that believeth not is condemned already, because he hath not believed in the name of the only begotten Son of God" (John 3:18). So plain a statement should forever silence the suggestion that what we believe is of little consequence.

2. *Convictions Which Make Christians*

When the New Testament is read thoughtfully, it must be recognized that the early churches tenaciously believed certain things and regarded these beliefs as tests of fellowship. The very fact that Christians were known as believers (Acts 5:14; 1 Tim. 4:12) is significant, while the declared purpose of one of the gospel writers is given in these words, "These are written, that ye might believe that Jesus is the Christ, the Son of God; and that believing ye might have life through his name" (John 20:31).

When the Philippian jailor, in a moment of spiritual emergency, asked Paul, "What must I do to be saved?" the prompt answer was, "Believe on the Lord Jesus Christ, and thou shalt be saved, and thy house" (Acts 16:30–31). The requirement was always belief, and the declared object of that belief was always Jesus Christ. Thus the Saviour's own plea was echoed by his anointed messengers, "This is the work of God, that ye believe on him whom he hath sent" (John 6:29).

3. *These Things Baptists Believe*

Although Baptists have consistently repudiated man-made creeds, they have as steadfastly upheld the New Testament as the authoritative source of Christian doctrine and practice. They have fought strenuously for freedom of belief for others, but have circumscribed their own liberty in the conviction that they have only one teacher, the Holy Spirit, and that his textbook is the Bible.

That those who seek membership in a Baptist church

should subscribe to Baptist belief is both right and reasonable. This is not to say that the new convert, who may be a child, should be expected to know and understand everything that Baptists believe. Neither is it to say that all Baptists believe alike or that they require complete conformity of doctrine from others. Baptists believe in the right of individual interpretation of the Scriptures under the leadership of the Holy Spirit. But are there not certain basic requirements of belief without which none should be considered qualified for acceptance into the fellowship of a Baptist church?

(1) *There is need for right belief about self and sin.*— The early preachers of the gospel placed the emphasis on repentance and faith because the first step toward the acceptance of Christ as Saviour is the recognition of one's need as a sinner. The good news is that "while we were yet sinners, Christ died for us" (Rom. 5:8). We must take our place as transgressors against God's laws, that we may know the blessedness of forgiveness.

(2) *There is need for right belief about Christ and his salvation.*—The apostle Paul expressed his belief in words as forceful as they are few, when he wrote, "The Son of God, who loved me, and gave himself for me" (Gal. 2:20). There can be no Christianity without the cross. Every Christian must be able to say, "He died for me." Eternity will be required for us to explore the full meaning of Calvary; but there can be no beginning to Christian experience without the acknowledgment that "God so loved the world, that he gave his only begotten Son, that whosoever believeth in him should not perish, but have everlasting life" (John 3:16).

(3) *There is need for right belief about the church and its ordinances.*—No beginner in the Christian life should be expected to be acquainted with every aspect of the doctrines of baptism and the Lord's Supper. But by their

rejection of infant baptism and by their use of the term "believer's baptism," Baptists imply the necessity for an intelligent, voluntary participation in that ordinance. All who present themselves for membership in a Baptist church need to have an understanding of what baptism and the Lord's Supper signify. To be lacking such knowledge is to miss the joy of obedience to Christ, identification with Christ, and witness for Christ. The church has an unescapable responsibility to instruct its new members in these things. To that end it conducts its Training Union. When the Ethiopian eunuch stepped from the baptismal pool, we are told that "he went on his way rejoicing." So should it be with all who, in awareness of what they are doing, pass through the same waters.

4. *Growth Through Knowledge*

The believer's experience of Christ is intended to be one of constant enrichment through increasing knowledge. The joy of salvation is not an end but a beginning. In his parable of the vine, Jesus indicated the necessity for growth and fruit bearing on the part of the Christian, adding: "These things have I spoken unto you, that my joy might remain in you, and that your joy might be full" (John 15:11). The way to keep the joy which Christ brings into the redeemed life, and to add to that joy, is to grow spiritually and be fruitful.

God has made adequate provision for Christian development. By the regular reading of the Bible, by the practice of prayer, by participation in the work and worship of the church, and by fellowship with other Christians, we may exercise our spiritual muscles and advance toward spiritual maturity. If we neglect these things, we must not be surprised if our Christianity loses its luster and what God intends to be a foretaste of heaven becomes unsatisfying and commonplace. Of Christian living and

church membership it is true that the more we give to
them the more we shall get from them.

The Training Union exists to emphasize the necessity
for Christian growth and to furnish means toward its at-
tainment. The weekly programs of the Training Union
give instruction to the believer for his own personal life,
for his better understanding of New Testament doctrine,
for his deepening appreciation of Baptist history, for his
knowledge of our denominational organization, and for
his wider vision of world missionary needs and endeavors.
Also, by its requirement of daily, personal devotions (Bible reading and prayer) the Training Union fosters the
spiritual development of church members by means
which God has ordained to reach "the measure of the
stature of the fulness of Christ" (Eph. 4:13). The Training Union also emphasizes service as a means of spiritual
growth. Just as physical development and health contribute to the enjoyment of life, so spiritual development
and health produce in the Christian that fruit of the
Spirit which includes "love, joy, peace" (Gal. 5:22).

IV. CHRISTLIKE BEHAVIOR

1. *Belief and Behavior Inseparable*

When certain of the Pharisees and Sadducees presented
themselves to John for baptism, our Lord's great fore-
runner said, "Who hath warned you to flee from the
wrath to come? Bring forth therefore fruits meet for repentance" (Matt. 3:7–8). Later, in his Sermon on the
Mount, Jesus himself declared, "Not every one that saith
unto me, Lord, Lord, shall enter into the kingdom of
heaven; but he that doeth the will of my Father which is
in heaven" (Matt. 7:21).

The close connection between belief and behavior is
indicated throughout the Scriptures. James goes so far as

to say that it is useless to talk about belief (faith) unless it is interpreted in behavior (works): "As the body without the spirit is dead, so faith without works is dead also" (James 2:26).

2. *Evidence of Regeneration*

New Christians are received for baptism by our churches upon their profession of faith in Christ as their Saviour, just as it was done in New Testament days. Every precaution that is possible should be taken by the pastor and all personal workers, through instruction and questions, to be sure that each one has had a genuine experience of conversion.

Immediately following baptism, each new Christian should join the pastor's class in a study of the book, *Your Life and Your Church,* by James L. Sullivan. Any new member who has not really accepted Christ may still be led to do so in this study, and all new members may get the right start in their church membership here.

It is certain that those who have the witness in their own hearts of the transforming grace of God drink deeply of that joy which the Father dispenses to his children.

The psalmist was overflowing with gratitude to God for his grace when he wrote, "He brought me up also out of an horrible pit, out of the miry clay, and set my feet upon a rock, and established my goings" (Psalm 40:2). Paul exulted in the thought of what the Lord had done with and for him when he wrote, "I thank Christ Jesus our Lord, who hath enabled me, for that he counted me faithful, putting me into the ministry; who was before a blasphemer, and a persecutor, and injurious" (1 Tim. 1:12–13). And to the Ephesian church this same apostle wrote, "And you hath he quickened, who were dead in trespasses and sins; wherein in time past ye walked according to the course of this world, ... and were by nature the children of wrath, even as others. But God, who is rich in mercy, for his great love wherewith he loved us, even when we were dead in sins, hath quickened us together with Christ, (by grace are ye saved;) and hath raised us up together, and made us sit together in heavenly places in Christ Jesus" (Eph. 2:1–6).

To recognize the handiwork of God in our lives, saving us from sin, making us new creatures, adopting us into his family, honoring us with assignments in his kingdom, qualifying us for membership in his church, is to discover reasons for joy abounding. No wonder Paul exhorted his Philippian friends, "Rejoice in the Lord alway: and again I say, Rejoice" (Phil. 4:4).

SUGGESTED TOPICS FOR DISCUSSION

1. What measures should a church take to insure that those who present themselves for membership have been converted?

2. Should a person's belief be made a test for church membership? State some fundamental New Testament beliefs.

3. Review the Training Union's contribution toward Christian growth.

OUTLINE

I. SAVING FAITH

1. The Practice of the Jerusalem Church
2. The Teaching of the Apostles
3. A Distinctive of Baptists

II. WILLING OBEDIENCE

1. The Master's Commission
2. New Testament Procedure
3. The Significance of Baptism
4. Is the Method Important?

III. RIGHT BELIEF

1. Does It Matter What We Believe?
2. Convictions which Make Christians
3. These Things Baptists Believe
    (1) There is need for right belief about self and sin.
    (2) There is a need for right belief about Christ and his salvation.
    (3) There is need for right belief about the church and its ordinances.
4. Growth through Knowledge

IV. CHRISTLIKE BEHAVIOR

1. Belief and Behavior Inseparable
2. Evidence of Regeneration

CHAPTER 3

Joy in Belonging

SOCIOLOGISTS tell us that human beings possess a gregarious instinct, which is their way of saying that we like to get together. Perhaps of all people in the world, this is specially true of Americans. Clubs, fraternities, societies, and fellowships abound in our country. We are great joiners, and we cheerfully pay the fees and subscriptions involved in order to belong to those organizations in which we and our friends are interested.

Such memberships bring satisfactions of various kinds. They are valuable to some because of the opportunity they afford for pursuing certain objects. To others, the chief attraction is in the social contacts which become possible: they feel that their membership enables them to meet the right kind of people. Another source of gratification may be the prestige which comes from belonging to select groups: membership, they feel, stamps upon them the hallmark of quality. For the high minded there is often pleasure in knowing that, by co-operation with others, they are enriching their service to mankind.

Perhaps the greatest satisfaction of all is the legitimate pride of the man who, by his membership, becomes part of an institution with a long and noble tradition of accomplishment. There is nothing of conceit in such pride. He knows full well that he can claim no credit for the magnificent story of the past. That belongs to other men —to pioneers of years gone by, and to faithful affiliates of successive generations who have maintained, and even added to, the splendid reputation of the institution with which he now finds himself associated. Thus pride is mixed with a proper humility and becomes a spur to dedication and endeavor. His ambition is to prove worthy of such antecedents and to carry the cause forward to further heights of recognition and success.

All of these satisfactions should be experienced to an even greater degree by the church member. They are part of the joy of belonging. If he fails to realize them, then to that extent he misses the blessing that God intends him to enjoy. But how can he appreciate the privileges of church membership unless he holds an exalted opinion of the church?

Lack of understanding of the character of the church surely explains why many people whose names are on church rolls treat their membership so lightly. A right concept of the church as to its divine origin, its relationship to the Lord Jesus Christ, its God-ordained mission, and its glorious destiny should thrill all of our hearts and impel a love and a loyalty which can be offered to no earthly organization. This is what Timothy Dwight tried to express when he wrote:

> I love Thy Church, O God!
> Her walls before Thee stand,
> Dear as the apple of Thine eye,
> And graven on Thy hand.
>
> For her my tears shall fall;
> For her my prayers ascend;
> To her my cares and toils be given,
> Till toils and cares shall end.
>
> Beyond my highest joy,
> I prize her heavenly ways,
> Her sweet communion, solemn vows,
> Her hymns of love and praise.

I. THE LORD OF THE CHURCH

Whose is the church? The Bible leaves us in no doubt as to the answer. Paul consistently used the phrase "the church of God," both in speaking and in writing (Acts 20:28; 1 Cor. 15:9; 1 Tim. 3:15). The first of these references, which is included in the apostle's farewell message to the elders of Ephesus, reads in its extended form: "Feed the church of God, which he hath purchased with his own blood." Some translators render this: "Feed the church of the Lord, which he hath purchased with his own blood." Others, perhaps interpreting the Greek idiom more correctly, make the words read: "Feed the church of God, which has been purchased by the blood of his Own." Either rendering is in harmony with the teaching of Ephesians 1:22, concerning Christ and the church, that God "hath put all things under his feet, and gave him to be the head over all things to the church."

The church is God's as, indeed, are all things. But God the Father has placed the church under the lordship of his Son. Not only is this so in the sense that by his unity with the Father he shares his prerogatives and powers; God has specifically and deliberately made Jesus head of the church in recognition of his unique relationship to the church which he purchased by the shedding of his blood. So, in speaking to his disciples at Caesarea Philippi, Jesus declared his proprietorship when he said: "Upon this rock I will build *my church*" (Matt. 16:18). God had already made over the title deeds to him, and soon he would endorse them with the crimson signature of the cross.

1. *Christ the Founder of the Church*

Many noble institutions of this world draw much of their fame and prestige from revered founders. Often, like

Johns Hopkins University, they bear the name of their original benefactor. Washington and Lee University has memorialized in its name both a generous gift to the school from the first President of the United States and the inspired, self-sacrificing leadership which it received for six years from Robert E. Lee. It is not an uncommon thing for statues and other suitable monuments to be erected to the memory of such pioneers and helpers. These may be prompted by admiration or gratitude; but are they not also demonstrations of pride, furnished by those who feel that they have entered into a glorious heritage and are themselves honored even by distant association with such worthies of the past?

The church is linked historically, and in other ways possible only to an institution of its supernatural character, with Jesus Christ himself. He is the glorious founder of the church. It is a distortion of biblical statement, and an affront to the person and dignity of the divine Son of God, to claim this honor for any other. Whatever the words of Matthew 16:18 may mean ("Thou art Peter, and upon this rock I will build my church") they cannot and do not mean that the apostle Peter initiated the church. It is Christ's church in every sense: his as to conception; his as to constitution; his as to government; his as to ownership; his as to purpose and performance; his as to glorious consummation.

The question as to when the church began has exercised devout and scholarly minds down the Christian years. To fix a day and hour, and to say: "Before this there was no church, and at this point the church began," does not seem possible. Pentecost is often referred to as "the birthday of the church"; but this cannot be. Was not the church in existence in the upper room when "Jesus took bread, and blessed it, and brake it, and gave it to the disciples, and said, Take, eat; this is my body"? (Matt.

26:26). What did the Master mean when he said, "Tell
it unto the church" (Matt. 18:17) if there was no church
to which it could be told? In our uncertainty as to time
and place for the founding of the church, we can surely
say: Christ founded the church, and, when he said to men,
"Follow me," and they followed him—there was the
church.

It is sufficient that Christ founded the church. It is for
us to obey his teachings concerning it.

2. *Christ the Head of the Church*

As we have already seen, God has given the lordship of
the church to his Son who "loved the church, and gave
himself for it" (Eph. 5:25). This is a continuing lordship; that is, Christ is as much head of the church today
as when Paul wrote to the Colossians: "He is the head of
the body, the church: who is the beginning, the firstborn
from the dead; that in all things he might have the pre-
eminence" (Col. 1:18). Jesus has not abdicated in favor
of another, neither has he appointed a vice-regent, be he
pope, prelate, priest, or pastor.

There are some who find attraction and appeal in the
trappings of ecclesiastical office. They like to belong to
organizations which are controlled by men bearing high-
sounding titles, wearing expensive and elaborate vest-
ments, and surrounded by pomp and ceremony. But the
New Testament Christian who repudiates all such
sacerdotal pride and pretense actually professes the
highest churchmanship of all. For he acknowledges no authority within the church but that of Christ; and the
loyalty he owes is not to boards and presbyteries, not to
bishops and cardinals, but to the Son of God himself.
"Call no man your father upon the earth: for one is your
Father, which is in heaven. Neither be ye called masters:
for one is your Master, even Christ" (Matt. 23:9–10).

3. *Christ the Church's Bond of Unity*

The three principal figures used in the New Testament to illustrate the church's relationship to Christ are a body (1 Cor. 12:12; Eph. 1:22–23; 4:15–16), a building (Eph. 2:19–22), and a bride (Eph. 5:25–27). In each case, the first implied lesson concerns Christ's unshared priority in that relationship: He is to the church what the head is to a body, what the foundation is to a building, and what the husband is to a bride.

A second lesson, however, is concerned with unity within the church, a point which is interestingly developed in those passages which describe the church as a body and a building. As the various members of the body function harmoniously through their individual relationship to the head, and as the parts of a building hold together in usefulness and beauty through their dependence upon the foundation, so Christians are united in fellowship and service by their personal ties with the Lord Jesus Christ. As in the parable of the vine (John 15), oneness and usefulness are the result of abiding in Christ. That is true whether we think of ourselves as branches or bodies or bricks or brides.

Once again, such a conception of unity within the church dignifies the individual church member. We fulfil our true functions and we realize the highest in mutual fellowship as we strengthen the bonds of love and loyalty between ourselves and our Saviour. It is to be feared that many have not begun to think of such a sublime possibility as this. Their church membership is unexciting to them because it is regarded as a commonplace, instead of being accepted as the most exalted privilege earth knows.

Who can measure the abounding joys of meaningful church membership?

4. *Christ the Message of the Church*

Perhaps we have begun to understand something of what Paul meant when he wrote of Jesus that God "gave him to be the head over all things to the church" (Eph. 1:22). To think of the church is to think of Christ, for the church has no meaning, no mission, and no message apart from him.

The church has a message. That is one of the glorious things about it, enhancing the privilege and increasing the joy of membership. There are organizations which are self-contained and self-sufficient. They exist to study or promote matters of limited interest, and their membership is restricted and select. But the church of Jesus Christ has a message for all mankind. It is the message the world needs—the only message that can solve the problem of its sin, heal its divisions, secure the realization of its peace, and reconcile creation and Creator in perfect obedience and enduring love. Its message is a person, and that person is Christ.

The prophet Isaiah, anticipating the coming of the gospel, exclaimed: "How beautiful upon the mountains are the feet of him that bringeth good tidings, that publisheth peace; that bringeth good tidings of good, that publisheth salvation; that saith unto Zion, Thy God reigneth!" (Isa. 52:7). If you are a church member, that should mean you!

II. THE PURPOSE OF THE CHURCH

1. *A Fellowship of Believers*

The first thought of God concerning Adam, after he had placed him in the garden of Eden, was that he needed a companion. "The Lord God said, It is not good that the man should be alone; I will make him an helpmeet for

him" (Gen. 2:18). The same divine recognition of man's
social needs and of provision to that end was acknowledged by the psalmist when he wrote: "God setteth the
solitary in families" (Psalm 68:6). The home, the community, and the state are each an evidence of the fact that
men were not intended to live to themselves, and that
they can only realize the best in happiness and in achievement through association with others.

It is written of Jesus and his disciples: "He goeth up
into a mountain, and calleth unto him whom he would:
and they came unto him. And he ordained twelve, that
they should be with him" (Mark 3:13–14). It is surely
true that Jesus needed these men and that they needed
him. But they also needed one another, and by their
response to the Master's call they constituted themselves
a fellowship which was essential to the fulfilment of
Christ's program. Later, when they were ready to go as
his messengers, he "began to send them forth by two and
two" (Mark 6:7), thus indicating their dependence upon
one another—as well as upon those spiritual resources
which he promised—for the effective discharge of their
assignment.

In calling out his church, Christ had purposes of far-
reaching importance in the over-all program of his kingdom. Some of those purposes will only be fully revealed
and realized in eternity. But he had one immediate purpose which can and should be fulfilled in the present experience of each of us who profess to be his followers. He
knew our need for companionship and friendship on the
level of our own humanity, and he provided for that in
the institution of the church.

2. *A Depository of Truth*

There is nothing like responsiblity to bring the best
out of a person. If this is so, church membership should

make great characters of us all. For God had no little plan
in mind when he designed the church. He entrusted it
with his truth, and he relies upon it to guard that truth
at all costs and to pass it on unchanged and undimmed
from generation to generation.

The failure of the Jewish people demanded a new plan
that would not fail. God purposed that Abraham's children should be the vehicle for the revelation of himself to
all mankind. But they departed from the very truth with
which they had been so solemnly entrusted, and God, dis-
appointed but not defeated in his plans, turned elsewhere. "I will say to them which were not my people,
Thou art my people; and they shall say, Thou art my
God" (Hos. 2:23). God set the church at the very heart
of his program, and through it he will bring to pass all
that his justice and his mercy demand.

Nobody had a higher conception of the church's task
than Paul. His own life was disciplined and constrained
at every point by the realization that to the church, and
to him as messenger of the church, God had committed
the gospel of his love. "Now then we are ambassadors for
Christ, as though God did beseech you by us: we pray you
in Christ's stead, be ye reconciled to God" (2 Cor. 5:20).

Paul thought of this entrustment not only in terms of
the evangel, but also as a body of doctrine (contained for
us in the Scriptures) which the church and its members
must preserve intact, proclaim in its fulness, and pass on
undiluted and untrimmed. "O Timothy," he wrote to a
young pastor, "keep that which is committed to thy trust"
(1 Tim. 6:20); and again: "Hold fast the form of sound
words, which thou hast heard of me, in faith and love
which is in Christ Jesus" (2 Tim. 1:13).

Every church member is God's trustee, charged with
the responsibility of knowing the truth for himself, teaching it to others (2 Tim. 2:2), and jealously guarding it

against its foes. Trusteeship, surely, has no loftier expression. The obligation is heavy, but the honor is incalculable. What a marvelous thing it is to be a church member!

3. *"A Royal Priesthood"*

Peter had in mind the words of Hosea 2:23, quoted in the preceding section, when he wrote: "Ye are a chosen generation; a royal priesthood, an holy nation, a peculiar people; that ye should show forth the praises of him who hath called you out of darkness into his marvellous light: which in time past were not a people, but are now the people of God: which had not obtained mercy, but now have obtained mercy" (1 Peter 2:9–10). Each of the phrases used by Peter to describe Christian believers had previously been used to describe Israel; and each of them, significantly enough, is used in a collective sense, not to apply to the individual as an individual, but to his association with other Christians in the membership of Christ's church.

This great statement of Peter's mentions a purpose of the church which is awesome in its high demand. Having described the church by four offices of great significance, he says that we are called to these offices "that ye should shew forth the praises of him who hath called you. . . ." (1 Peter 2:9). The church, then, exists for the praise and glory of God, a thought which is Paul's also, for he has written: "Unto him be glory in the church by Christ Jesus throughout all ages, world without end" (Eph. 3:21).

If our church programs were examined with this exalted idea in mind, should some items be eliminated from the list of activities? If the church exists for the glory of God we need to be scrupulous in our policies and promotion. The final test, after all, can never be negative: Is this or that consistent and right for a church of Jesus Christ?

Dues

The final test must be: Is everything that we do, on Sundays and weekdays, in every department of activity, contributing to the glory of our God?

But let us look at it this way. An invitation to join an organization which had as its purpose the advancement of the prestige of the United States would probably flatter us. It would appeal to our patriotism and summon us to endeavor and, if need be, to self-denial that the cause of our country might be helped. As church members we are already part of an institution which has the praise of God as its objective. Do we not pray, "Hallowed be thy name"? That is, we tell God that we earnestly desire that he shall be known and honored in an ever-increasing way and that his name may be reverenced above all other names. The church exists to answer that prayer. You and I, as members of the church, can help to answer it.

4. *A Witness to the World*

There is need to return to a Bible passage already quoted in order that we may complete it. Mark 3:14 reads: "He ordained twelve, that they should be with him," and continues: "and that he might send them forth." Jesus was not founding a cozy club when he began his church. He was fashioning an instrument of impelling purpose—a mighty company of men and women who, having become the beneficiaries of his love, would dedicate themselves to his service in seeking the redemption of other lives.

As church members we have a task to perform. We are not asked whether we will accept it. Christ called us into the fellowship of his church for this very purpose. If we are not prepared to be his witnesses, there is reason to doubt the reality of our conversation, for like Andrew telling Peter his brother, the very nature of the born-again child of God is to share his blessing with others.

And when we do, then the joy of church membership is experienced at its greatest and best, for nothing can bring such gladness to the Christian heart as to win another soul for Jesus.

III. THE STORY OF THE CHURCH

People travel from all parts of the world to visit the cathedrals of Europe. Not only are these buildings of surpassing beauty of design, but, in the majority of cases, they are rich in legend and in history, enabling the fortunate visitor to live again some of the most spectacular and dramatic events of the past. But it is not uncommon to find people living in the shadow of these famous shrines who have never been inside. They have only to cross the road to see what others come thousands of miles to look upon; but they are not interested. Somehow all the wonder of the place has passed them by; and architecture which charms and dazzles the visitors is to them just a heap of stones.

Some church members are like this. They belong to the church on the corner. It cost $50,000 to build it; it has 400 members; and its pastor's name is John Doe. That is about all they know. Ask them who founded their church, and they cannot say. Who was its first pastor? They don't know. Test them on a little denominational history, and they quickly reveal their ignorance. They have never been to an associational meeting or a state convention, perhaps not even to a church business meeting. As for reading the story of Baptist forerunners or missionary pioneers—that has never occurred to them. Is there any wonder that they find their church membership dull and uninspiring? What, after all, do they know about their church? As pride of country depends upon knowledge of its history, so joy in church membership requires some familiarity with the glorious record of the past.

1. *Years of Glorious Progress*

If all of us would sit down and read the Acts of the Apostles from beginning to end it would do something for us. Nothing more dramatic exists in the literature of the world. There was a Man crucified outside the walls of Jerusalem. He had a small group of followers, but the night before the final tragedy they all "forsook him, and fled." Some twenty years later, the magistrates of an important Greek city were alarmed to be told: "These that have turned the world upside down have come hither" (Acts 17:6). Two preachers of the crucified One had so shaken the world of their day that their reputation ran ahead of them. And before long, Jesus, the victim of the cross, had his followers in the very palace of Caesar in Rome (Phil. 4:22).

If we seek an explanation of this story of Christian conquest, we must turn to Acts 2 and the recorded fulfilment of the promise of Jesus to his disciples: "Ye shall receive power, after that the Holy Ghost is come upon you" (Acts 1:8). After returning to his Father's house, the Saviour bestowed upon his church the gift of his Spirit. Centuries before, this day of heavenly visitation had been anticipated, and God himself had said: "On my servants and on my handmaidens I will pour out in those days of my Spirit" (Acts 2:18). The day of Pentecost has gone, and its peculiar phenomenon will never be repeated. But "those days" are still with us, for the Spirit is still with us, and his power is available to every believer whose service through the church may still be like those who turned the world upside down.

2. *The Noble Army of Martyrs*

Memorial Day brings our nation to a two-minute act of remembrance in which we ask God to make America worthy of those who died in freedom's name. No cause has ever commanded such devotion as Christ's. Whole periods of the church's history must be written in blood, as the powers of evil offered resistance to the onward progress of the gospel and men in league with Satan sought in vain to extinguish the light by killing the torch-bearers.

Many of those heroic souls, both men and women, who laid down their lives rather than deny their Lord, are shadowy figures on history's page. History has preserved the names of some, but little more. Yet, while the details may be blurred, we know, from the evidence of friends and enemies, that hundreds died, burned like human torches, or thrown to the lions, for no other reason than their Christian faith. These were the church members of their day, whose loyalty rebukes us for our softness and challenges us to meet the conditions of our own times in the same spirit of fortitude and faith.

Dare we speak of joy as we consider the awful cruelties inflicted on these early Christians? They dared to do so. De Pressensé, historian of those days of terror, tells us: "The honour of suffering for the noblest of causes, the lively realization of that Divine support promised to all who are persecuted for the truth, the universal sympathy of the Church, the contrast between the horrors of the dungeon and the enthusiastic joy filling the heart of the captives, all contributed to raise the martyr Christians above themselves. They lived almost in a state of ecstacy."[1] Women went to their death in wedding garments, and old and young together entered the arena of execution singing Christian hymns.

> A noble army, men and boys,
> The matron and the maid,

[1] E. de Pressensé, *The Martyrs and Apologists* (London: Hodder and Stoughton, 1871), p. 87.

Around the Saviour's throne rejoice,
  In robes of light arrayed:
They climbed the steep ascent of heaven
  Through peril, toil, and pain;
O God, to us may grace be given
  To follow in their train.

—REGINALD HEBER

3. *Candles in the Dark*

Jesus himself foretold the opposition which would be offered to his gospel and the persecutions his followers would be called upon to endure. "Beware of men: for they will deliver you up to the councils, and they will scourge you in their synagogues; and ye shall be brought before governors and kings for my sake" (Matt. 10:17–18). More than that, he warned of the apostasy which would set in, asking the question, "When the Son of man cometh, shall he find faith on the earth?" (Luke 18:8).

After many years of enmity, the world began to offer its patronage to Christians, resulting in an alliance between church and state which all but extinguished the truth. The doctrines of the New Testament were obscured by false teachings promulgated by creeds and councils, and the practices of apostolic Christianity were superseded by a system of ritualism and priestcraft directed by one who claimed to be Christ's vice-regent on earth, the pope of Rome.

For several centuries, Christendom experienced the truth of those words of Jesus when he said, "If therefore the light that is in thee be darkness, how great is that darkness!" (Matt. 6:23). Superstition and ignorance prevailed. Magical rites were substituted for the simple ordinances of primitive Christianity. Intolerance and ecclesiastical tyranny did their utmost to destroy the gospel of salvation by faith. But for all this sinister effort, candles continued to glow in the dark. Brave souls, remaining loyal to their understanding of God's revelation in Christ, defied the combined authority of priests and emperors, and kept alive the flame of truth.

These nonconforming groups did not bear the name of Baptists, neither did they all agree at every point with what Baptists believe today. But we salute them across the centuries as brethren in the faith, through whose death-defying loyalty the true succession of New Testament churches was maintained.

4. *The Dawning of a New Day*

At length, a mighty blow was delivered against the powers of spiritual darkness. Under the leadership of Martin Luther (1483–1546), Europe was aroused to realize the perils of the Papacy, and by means of the Reformation a new emphasis was given to the glorious New Testament doctrines of grace. Many others contributed to this revival of Christian teaching and preaching: Wycliffe in England, Huss in Bohemia, Hubmaier in Germany, Calvin in Switzerland, and Knox in Scotland —men whom God raised up to kindle faith and hope in others' hearts, and who helped to scatter the mists of falsehood and unbelief which had for so long subdued the light of Christ's gospel.

Unfortunately, however, the Reformation stopped short of a complete restoration of New Testament church order and practice. Some errors and abuses of the Romish system were corrected, but some remnants of its teaching and ritual were retained. Here and there courageous voices were raised calling for the repudiation of such unscriptural and superstitious survivals as infant baptism. But the leadership of the Reformation turned a deaf ear to these pleas and even persecuted those who gave expression to them.

God still needed a faithful remnant who would cherish

the faith and practice of the early church, stripped of all
the accretions of ecclesiasticism. And the remnant was
there, ready to burn or to drown if need be but unwill-
ing to silence its testimony whatever the consequences.
In this struggle for truth, individuals and groups emerged
with whom Baptists proudly claim kinship. We honor
those who by their doctrinal integrity and endurance under persecution sought to maintain a New Testament witness throughout the centuries.

5. *Our Baptist Heritage*

In England and on the continent of Europe, God found
his stalwarts who were ready to defy church or state, or
both together, rather than submit to the suppression of
their testimony. Early in the seventeenth century, first in
Holland and then in England, the name Baptist began to
be used by groups who had lit their torches at the flame
which God had kept alight throughout the centuries of
religious compromise and apostasy. John Smythe was first
to put into writing the great principle that every man has
a right to complete religious liberty. "Christ only is the
King," he affirmed, "and lawgiver of the church and con-
science."

We stay only long enough to salute the memory of such
men, and then change the century and the scene, trans-
ferring our admiration from Baptists in England to Baptists in Virginia. Over one hundred years had passed
since the first pioneers of our faith raised the standard of
New Testament Christianity and religious freedom on
America's shores. Successors of these early preachers had
made their way southward; and in Virginia they took
their stand against the intolerance of church and state.
Beginning in 1766, forty-two Baptist ministers were put
into jail for their convictions, but faithfulness and cour-
age brought their reward. Before the turn of the century,

America had written the Bill of Rights into her constitution, the first statement of which declares: "Congress shall make no law respecting an establishment of religion, or prohibiting the free exercise thereof."

6. *Southern Baptists Today*

As church members, we have entered into the heritage secured by the loyalty and self-sacrifice of those who have gone before. We should be proud of our Baptist story, and of the names which give it luster—John Bunyan, Felix Mantz, Balthasar Hubmaier, Roger Williams, William Carey, Charles Haddon Spurgeon, and a host of others. No group of people follow in a more glorious succession than twentieth-century Baptists, and none have a greater destiny to fulfil.

Today, Baptists are to be found in all parts of the world, a mighty force for righteousness over twenty million strong. Of this number, over eighteen million live in the United States, and almost half of these (8,169,491) are members in Southern Baptist churches (1955).

The growth of Southern Baptists is one of the most impressive factors in modern American religious life. First organized as a separate denomination in 1845, Southern Baptists then had 4,126 churches with a membership of 351,951. It took twenty-seven years for this membership to reach its first million, and another thirty-four to arrive at the next million. In the second decade of this century, however, rapid strides were made—a period marked by a new emphasis on the Sunday school and by the introduction of the Training Union as an integral part of each church program. Baptisms increased from year to year, and in three recent years numbered more than one million. There are now more than 30,000 Southern Baptist churches, contributing through their offerings, nearly six million dollars every Sunday to kingdom causes.

To think of this vast fellowship of Baptist people, and to be able to say, "I belong," is surely one of life's greatest privileges. Of the corresponding responsibilities which this involves more shall be said; but, for the present, we may surely thank God for our church membership which links us with a glorious past and with a present opportunity unsurpassed in this world.

SUGGESTED TOPICS FOR DISCUSSION

1. What three principal figures does the New Testament use to describe the relationship between Christ and the church? Discuss their significance.

2. "Every church member is God's trustee." Discuss this statement.

3. Review the growth of Southern Baptists since 1845.

OUTLINE

I. THE LORD OF THE CHURCH

   1. Christ the Founder of the Church

   2. Christ the Head of the Church

   3. Christ the Church's Bond of Unity

   4. Christ the Message of the Church

II. THE PURPOSE OF THE CHURCH

   1. A Fellowship of Believers

   2. A Depository of Truth

   3. "A Royal Priesthood"

   4. A Witness to the World

III. THE STORY OF THE CHURCH

   1. Years of Glorious Progress

   2. The Noble Army of Martyrs

   3. Candles in the Dark

   4. The Dawning of a New Day

   5. Our Baptist Heritage

   6. Southern Baptists Today

CHAPTER 4

Joy in Worship

AN EXILE FROM HOME, unable to continue his practice of regular attendance at God's house, wrote two of the most beautiful of the psalms. This is how he began: "As the hart panteth after the water brooks, so panteth my soul after thee, O God" (Psalm 42:1). Then, as he thought of his plight as a prisoner in a distant country, he added: "My soul thirsteth for God, for the living God: when shall I come and appear before God?" He was inclined to discouragement and self-pity as he thought of others still privileged to attend worship services; but he comforted himself with the memory of those days when he, too, was a worshiper. "I had gone with the multitude," he said, "I went with them to the house of God, with the voice of joy and praise, with a multitude that kept holyday." And finally, after alternating moods of hope and despair, he made this his prayer: "O send out thy light and thy truth: let them lead me; let them bring me unto thy holy hill, and to thy tabernacles. Then will I go unto the altar of God, unto God my exceeding joy: yea, upon the harp will I praise thee, O God my God" (Psalm 43:3–4).

How much does God's house mean to us? Do we enjoy attending worship services? Do we anticipate Sunday with pleasure and answer the call of the church bells with a sense of privilege and high expectation? Do we thrill to the sight of a church auditorium filled with worshiping people? Are we carried along by the service as it proceeds, conscious that we have a part in its offering of praise and thanksgiving, and blessed by the realization of God's presence among his people? Do we feel, when the service is over and the benediction has been pronounced, that some deep need of our nature has been satisfied, and that we are more ready to meet the demands of a new week because we have worshiped?

Perhaps many people, church members included, would have to give negative answers to some, if not all, of these questions. They "go to church" because they regard it as a duty—in some communities, a sort of social obligation. But they could (and do) miss church attendance without being aware of any loss. At the slightest excuse, they absent themselves from God's house; and, unless something happens to change their attitude, they are likely to drift away altogether. When they are in church, they sit passively in their seats, remain silent when others sing, let their minds wander to the consideration of irrelevancies during the pastoral prayer, and doze their way through the sermon. They may in courtesy tell the minister that he brought a good message; but, if he asked them what his text was, they would be terribly embarrassed.

Worship is too significant, too rich in potential blessing for the participant, and too important in the total plan of God for his people for its values to be passed up in this way. Therefore, in this chapter, we shall consider the subject of worship: what it is, how we engage in it, what are the benefits we should seek from it, and what part it plays in the intentions of God himself, who is the object of our worship.

I. THE MEANING OF WORSHIP

1. *The Broken Contact*

God made us beings capable of fellowship with himself. Of all creation, men alone bear the image of their

Maker, for God gave to men something of his likeness
(Gen. 1:26–27) so that he might honor them with his
friendship and receive their love and obedience in return.
In the cool of the day, we are told, he walked in the garden of Eden—not once, we may surely believe, but often;
and, as the man and the woman who owed him their all
were blessed by his presence, he also found something in
their company which brought joy and satisfaction to his
heart.

But one day Adam failed to keep his appointment, and
God walked the paths of Paradise calling, "Where art
thou?" Alas, he knew the answer. Man had sinned, and
the bond of fellowship had been broken. Instead of being
welcomed with an eager greeting, God was met with a
stony silence, broken only by the pitiful excuses of one
who had fallen into disobedience, bringing upon his head
the penalty of banishment from the divine presence.

Some philosophies of religion teach that humanity's
story is one of progress from darkness to light, primitive
superstition being the original element from which, by
dint of his own effort and inquiry, man has climbed to
nobler spiritual concepts. The Bible does not so teach.
Paul epitomized the history of the race when he wrote:
"They are without excuse: because that, when they knew
God, they glorified him not as God, neither were thankful; but became vain in their imaginations, and their foolish heart was darkened. Professing themselves to be wise,
they became fools, and changed the glory of the uncor-
ruptible God into an image made like to corruptible man,
and to birds, and fourfooted beasts, and creeping things.
Wherefore God also gave them up. . . ." (Rom. 1:20–24).

2. *A God-shaped Vacuum*

It has been expressively said that the admittance of sin,
with the consequent forfeiture of fellowship with the

divine, left a God-shaped vacuum in the human heart. How men have tried to fill that vacuum makes up the story of religions. The sin of Eden has been repeated again and again as men have rejected the light which has shone from heaven, and, turning their backs upon the true God, have bowed down to idols of their own devising. Even Israel, chosen by Jehovah to be his peculiar people, profaned his holy name and followed the idolatrous and ofttimes immoral practices of their heathen neighbors. Because man is a worshiping being he must either acknowledge the true God or find an alternative.

It seems to be the teaching of the apostle Paul that the devil has exploited this trait of human nature for his own ends. "Now the Spirit speaketh expressly, that in the latter times some shall depart from the faith, giving heed to seducing spirits, and doctrines of devils" (1 Tim. 4:1). A very meager knowledge of the abominations which have been practiced in the name of religion compels the conclusion that Satan himself has played a big part in deceiving mankind with false faiths which, instead of helping men toward God, act as opiates on their spiritual sensibilities. Even the nobler forms of religion which men have followed have proved to be substitutes for God rather than steppingstones toward him.

3. *The Answer of Revelation*

There have been hungry hearts, however, that have cried, "Oh that I knew where I might find him!" (Job 23:3). And God has not been indifferent to their cry. The knowledge of things divine, which was forfeited through human sin, has been made available by the initiative of God. We speak of this unveiling of truth as "revelation," making a distinction between the revealed religion of the Scriptures and those natural religions which at best are only substitutes for ultimate truth.

The writer to the Hebrews summed up the story of God's self-revelation in the introductory words of his epistle. "God, who at sundry times and in divers manners spake in time past unto the fathers by the prophets, hath in these last days spoken unto us by his Son" (Heb. 1:1–2). To men like Abraham, Moses, David, Elijah, and Isaiah, to mention but a few, God made himself known, charging them with the responsibility of communicating to others the eternal truths that were entrusted to them. By the spoken and written word they discharged their responsibility; and the record of their adventure of faith is inscribed for us in the pages of the Old Testament. It is significant to note that each of these men was a worshiper. The knowledge of God that came to them drove them to their knees in wonder, love, and praise.

Of these Old Testament worthies it is said that they "received not the promise: God having provided some better thing for us, that they without us should not be made perfect" (Heb. 11:39–40). That better thing is the gospel, brought to us by God's own Son, enabling us to say: "God, who commanded the light to shine out of darkness, hath shined in our hearts, to give the light of the knowledge of the glory of God in the face of Jesus Christ" (2 Cor. 4:6).

4. *The Response of Grateful Hearts*

What we learn about God in the Bible and through the person of his Son, our Saviour, inspires our worship. The attributes of God—his might, his wisdom, his creative skill, his omniscience, his holiness—these summon us to wondering adoration. The realization of his providential care excites our gratitude, for "in him we live, and move, and have our being" (Acts 17:28). But the supreme stimulus to worship is the knowledge of God's redeeming love for men. "In this was manifested the love of God toward us, because that God sent his only begotten Son into the world, that we might live through him. Herein is love, not that we loved God, but that he loved us, and sent his Son to be the propitiation for our sins" (1 John 4:9–10).

It is not surprising that the Book which reveals God to us is the greatest treatise on worship that was ever compiled. The inevitable response of men to the unveiling of God in his majesty and mercy is worship. So it was in the Old Testament, which tells how tabernacle and Temple were built to provide a symbol and a center for God's worshiping people. So it was in the gospel story, for after the disciples realized that their Master was "the Christ, the Son of the living God," beholding him "carried up into heaven. . . . they worshipped him, and returned to Jerusalem with great joy" (Luke 24:51–52). So, moreover, it is foretold for the glorious future, when the redeemed of every nation shall gather around the eternal throne, and shall worship him "that liveth for ever and ever" (Rev. 5:14).

> Praise Him ever,
> Bounteous Giver!
> Praise Him, Father, Friend, and Lord!
> Each glad soul its free course winging,
> Each glad voice its free song singing,
> Praise the great and mighty Lord!
> —J. S. BLACKIE

II. THE MANNER OF WORSHIP

For the Christian, the worship of God is not an elective —something he may do, or not do, as his fancy leads. Those who excuse themselves from worship, or dictate how and where their worship shall be offered, repudiate the very spirit of worship by their attitude. Worship means nothing if it does not involve obedience; and, if gratitude be its motive, then obedience will be cheerfully rendered.

1. *A Place Provided*

It is true that worship can be offered anywhere and at any time, and circumstances may compel the child of God to fulfil the obligation of worship in strange places and at odd hours. But it is equally true that those who glibly talk about worshiping God as well on the golf course as in church usually do not worship at all. Doubtless the Lord recognized this frailty of our natures when he gave commandment first for the tabernacle, and then for the Temple, as places in which his people should worship him.

When our Lord said to the Samaritan woman: "The hour cometh, when ye shall neither in this mountain, nor yet at Jerusalem, worship the Father" (John 4:21), he was not suggesting that a place for worship was unimportant, but he was intimating that, under the dispensation of the gospel, there would cease to be a one and only center for worship. His own practice of regular attendance at the synagogue and the Temple, and the continuation of this practice by his apostles, emphasizes the necessity for a definite gathering place. When Jewish enmity excluded Christians from their congregations, worship was continued in the homes of believers, until increasing numbers made special buildings necessary. The impressive fact is that, in spite of difficulties and even under persecution, those who loved the Lord met to honor his name in places designated for the purpose. "Let us consider one another to provoke unto love and to good works," wrote the author of Hebrews to a sorely-tried company of Christians, adding significantly, "not forsaking the assembling of ourselves together, as the manner of some is; but exhorting one another: and so much the more, as ye see the day approaching" (Heb. 10:24–25).

Many of us have beautiful church houses to which we can go Sunday by Sunday. Will it be necessary for us to lose these before we appreciate the privilege that is ours? Such a disaster has befallen Christian congregations in many parts of the world, where, as the result of war, church buildings have been destroyed in large numbers. God has given American Christians finer church buildings than any other people in any other land. We have abundant reason for gratitude, and should see to it that these church houses are used for the high purposes for which they are intended.

2. *A Time Appointed*

God has ordained that one day in seven shall be dedicated to him. The Jews of our Lord's time, misunderstanding the spirit and purpose of the sabbath, had so multiplied the rules of its observance as to make the day a burden. Against this abuse of one of the beneficent provisions of the divine law Jesus hurled his protests (Matt. 12:1-13); but not a word that he said can be construed as meaning that his followers are to treat every day the same and so fail to give God his recurring seventh day in the calendar of life.

By apostolic practice, under the leadership of the Holy Spirit, the Jewish sabbath was superseded by the Lord's Day, so that Christians now observe their day of worship at the beginning and not at the end of each week. Meaningless prohibitions and restrictions which were imposed on sabbath keepers have been discarded by Christians. Doubtless the process of liberalization has gone much further than our Master intended, until today we have so stripped Sunday of its distinctives that the only difference between it and the other six days of the week is that on Sunday most people have a holiday.

Surely, the way to put joy into the Lord's Day is not to

secularize it but to sanctify it. If our hearts are right with our Lord, Sunday will be the gladdest day of seven because of the opportunity it affords for worship and for service in his name. We will recognize it as a wonderful provision that, in the midst of our busy world, God has set apart one day each week when we may employ ourselves in divine things, attending to the needs of our spiritual natures, taking time out to direct our thoughts Godward, and seeking opportunities to discharge our debt of love to our Heavenly Father in tasks undertaken in his name for the good of others.

3. *A Method Prescribed*

Old Testament worshipers knew exactly what was required of them when they attended the tabernacle or the Temple. At appointed times there were sacrifices to be brought and tithes to be offered; but, for the most part, the worshipers remained silent while the priests and choristers engaged in the ritual of worship. There seem to have been congregational responses in some of the services (1 Chron. 16:36; Jer. 33:11; Psalm 26:12); but so reliable an authority as Edersheim says that in our Lord's time Temple worshipers had no part beyond a responsive amen.

(1). *The Old Testament superseded.*—The most important and significant of the Temple rituals were discharged by the priests only, and some were the sole prerogative of the high priest. The outer court of the sacred area was the only portion to which the worshipers were admitted. The priests had access to the holy place, and the high priest to the holy of holies; the rest must wait outside while these discharged their solemn rituals, and returned.

With the coming of Christ all of this was changed, because in him all had fulfilment. After his sacrifice on

Calvary, none other was needed, for as God's perfect Lamb he made full and final atonement for sin. After he had gone into his Father's presence with the marks of his passion still upon him, no barrier could remain between the redeemed soul and its God: the holiest of all was open to those who came pleading the Saviour's name (Heb. 10:19–22).

(2). *"In spirit and in truth."*—The message of the New Testament is that Mosaic rite and ceremonial have fulfilled their purpose and are therefore discontinued. They were the "shadow of good things to come" (Heb. 10:1). Instead of worshiping God through symbols and by proxy, Christians are called upon to worship "in spirit and in truth" (John 4:24). The presence of God is no longer to be realized through material representation, even as historically sacred and significant as the ark of the covenant, but through spiritual fellowship; instead of a religion of the eyes and of the ears we have a religion of the heart. And in place of figures pointing on to reality (each slain lamb, for example, anticipating the "Lamb of God, which taketh away the sin of the world") we have the reality itself—"Jesus Christ the same yesterday, and today, and for ever." What is better, the shadow or the substance? The answer is obvious. How greatly advantaged we are to have been born this side of Bethlehem and Calvary and the first Easter morning! And how eagerly we should avail ourselves of the privilege of worship in which every worshiper is his own priest with equal access into the holy presence of Almighty God!

(A word of warning—reluctantly added, but undeniably necessary: There is constant danger of our return to what Paul calls "the weak and beggarly elements"—the outward trappings of religion, things which we can see and handle and smell, at the expense of spiritual values. The simpler the forms of worship we follow, the nearer they are to the New Testament pattern. Should we not strive for dignity without formality, for reverence without ritual, and for beauty without ostentation?)

(3). *Prayer, praise, and preaching.*—New Testament worship consists of three principal elements—prayer, praise, and preaching. Each of these should be a shared experience, participated in by everyone present. But this is not easily achieved, and because it is not easy many do not make the attempt and accordingly miss the blessing. It might be a good thing for our churches if we had instruction courses on how to worship.

a. Prayer.—Prayer may be engaged in individually or in groups. For Christian people, it is a natural expression of their fellowship for them to want to pray together. They have so much in common—needs, reasons for gratitude, and aspirations—that it is a fit and proper thing for them to unite their hearts in prayer (see Acts 5:31; 12:12; 13:3). Nothing but hopeless confusion would result, however, if each person in a congregation was to give utterance to his own prayer. Is it not more appropriate that the pastor of a church should lead his people to the throne of grace? Knowing many of their individual circumstances, he can embody in his prayer petitions which match their needs. From his familiarity with the program of the church and the kingdom he can ask God's blessing on all phases of the work. And out of his knowledge of the condition of the world around he can direct the thoughts of his congregation in interceding with the Lord for those who raise no prayers of their own. But the individual worshiper must concentrate upon the petitions that are offered, identifying himself with them in his heart and mind, and sealing everything with his own amen, whether audibly spoken or quietly breathed into the ear of God. This way there is joy in worship.

b. Praise.—Praise should form a great part of every exercise of worship. The Jewish people used the psalms to express their feelings of gratitude and adoration, and in many churches these unparalleled poems of spiritual yearning and devotion are still used. It was inevitable, however, that Christian worshipers should seek hymns and sacred songs which employ terms more familiar to them and embody language conforming more nearly to Christian experience and desire. We are blessed with a rich inheritance of hymnody by using which we can offer thanksgiving and prayer to God in words of rare beauty and spiritual power. But here again, participation by every worshiper is necessary if congregational singing is to achieve its purpose. There are undoubted values to be found in listening to God's praise sung by a trained choir. But for real joy in worship, few things are more helpful than lifting our voices in unison to the praise of our triune God.

"Give unto the Lord the glory due unto his name: bring an offering, and come into his courts." So reads Psalm 96:8. We praise God when we give of our substance; and the joy of an adequate stewardship has no equal in the experience of the worshiper. Instead of the offering being a sort of interlude in the order of worship, we should be careful to make it an occasion for personal dedication and for prayer that God would guide his people in the administration of consecrated money so that it may achieve the greatest good for the greatest number.

c. Preaching.—Baptists firmly believe that preaching belongs to true worship. The reading and exposition of God's Word together occupy the larger amount of time in most of our worship services. It should be scarcely necessary to say that those who do not listen will obtain little help from the ministry of the pulpit; yet there are many who miss much of the blessing, both Sunday morning and Sunday evening, because they pay scant attention to what is said. Heavy responsibility rests upon the preacher to bring messages which are of spiritual import. But no less responsibility is upon his congregation to give heed to the Word of life, seeking its values for themselves, and silently praying that God will use the presentation of his gospel to bring lost souls into the benefits of his salvation.

(4). *A service of memorial.*—The two ordinances of the New Testament church are usually observed during the worship service, and both have their contribution to make to the spiritual advantage of every worshiper. Since baptism has already been discussed, we confine ourselves here to a brief reference to the observance of the Lord's Supper.

The frequency of the observance of the Lord's Supper varies among Baptist churches, some holding it monthly, and some only once a quarter. Whenever it is held, it requires the attendance of every church member, in obedience to our Lord's command. No service should mean more to Christian people than this simple memorial service. It is not an occasion for the confession of sin; that should precede our coming to the table. It is not primarily an opportunity for fellowship, though the sense of family relationship should be strong among those who partake of the same meal. But the Supper of our Lord is supremely a call to wondering adoration. We hear our Saviour say: "This is my body which is given for you. . . . This cup is the new testament in my blood, which is shed for you," and gratefully we declare, in the words of the hymn:

> Thy presence makes the feast;
> Now let our spirits feel
> The glory not to be expressed,
> The joy unspeakable.
>
> —CHARLES WESLEY

III. THE MINISTRY OF WORSHIP

G. Campbell Morgan has said that the height of worship is realized in the use of two words which have never been translated—hallelujah and amen. Both of these words were constantly on the lips of Hebrew worshipers, the former as a formula of praise, hallelujah meaning "Praise ye the Lord," and amen being a term of assent, "So be it." True worship, according to this thought, consists of acknowledgment of the divine perfections and submission to the divine will.

1. *Giving Glory to God*

Many of the psalms consist of pure praise. Taking as samples Psalms 96–100, 103–108, and 145–150 we find an entire absence of petition, the sole object of the worshiper being adoration and thanksgiving. The language used is that of people taken out of themselves and introduced to the limitless universe in which God reigns supreme. For the time being they have forgotten their little worlds of mingled pain and pleasure. Their eyes are fixed on higher things, and the words they utter have lost the mark of the commonplace for they speak of the eternal throne and of him who sits thereon.

Are we in danger of losing the capacity for worship after this order? So many things crowd into the program of our church services that it is possible for the most important to become crowded out. There is a voice which bids us, "Be still, and know that I am God" (Psalm 46: 10). If it was necessary in more leisurely days to shift the focus of life from everyday cares and occupations to the contemplation of God, it is surely still more necessary for us.

Much of the joy of worship can come from a rekindling of our appreciation of the greatness of God. Here, surely, we have an advantage over worshipers of olden times. The results of scientific inquiry and research have revealed a universe more amazing than we can comprehend. A Vanderbilt University professor, for example, has suggested that the star which led the magi to Bethlehem was a supernova, thousands of light years away. God sparked it into brilliance, perhaps in the days of Abraham, arranging that it should become visible on earth at a time coinciding with the birth of the Saviour. The very suggestion thrills the worshiping heart with insights into the marvels of creation and the miracles of grace.

Those glimpses of the eternal state which we find in the Bible describe hosts of angels and of the redeemed giving praise to God and to the Lamb. Heaven will be a wonderful place for praise. But why wait for heaven? One man resolved: "As for me, I will come into thy house in the multitude of thy mercy" (Psalm 5:7). There is no better way to come. Let us count our blessings and we will be sure to find cause for praise. Then, in happy fellowship with other Christians, we will discover a new meaning in such great hymns as G. W. Conder's:

> All things praise Thee, Lord most high,
> Heaven and earth and sea and sky,
> All were for Thy glory made,
> That Thy greatness, thus displayed,
> Should all worship bring to Thee:
> All things praise Thee: Lord, may we.

2. *Enriching the Worshiper*

(1). *Worship emphasizes reality.*—We live in a material world in which tangible things tend to assume an exclusive importance. Making money is a legitimate occupation, but it can become an obsession so demanding as to leave no room for life's finer things. Even the pursuit of education may so absorb a person's time as to create

the impression that life affords nothing more important.
Our homes ought to command our affection and interest;
but there is such a thing as becoming so house-proud that
we have no horizons beyond the comfort and beauty of
our domestic furnishings. We need to be constantly reminded that reality does not consist in the things we
handle and see, but in the invisible and the spiritual.
Worship lifts our eyes from earthly levels and fixes them
on heaven; and in the quiet of God's house we adjust our
values and take stock of things in the light of eternity.

(2). *Worship brings understanding.*—God reserves
some of his choicest blessings for those who worship him
in ways which he has commanded. Long ago, a troubled
heart discovered the solution to its problem in the peace
of God's house. "When I thought to know this," the
psalmist wrote of his perplexity, "it was too painful for
me; until I went into the sanctuary of God; then understood I . . . " (Psalm 73:16–17). Thousands have had a
similar experience. They have gone to the place of worship carrying burdens of anxiety, sorrow, or indecision.
But in the service of prayer and praise, and in listening
to God's Word, they have found relief.

With that touch of genius which is so often found in
The Pilgrim's Progress, Bunyan tells us that it was "on
Saturday about midnight" that Christian and Hopeful,
prisoners of Giant Despair in Doubting Castle, "began to
pray, and continued in prayer till almost break of day."
Deliverance came to them on Sunday morning, the day
and the time when it has come to many others who were
prisoners of doubt or of fear or even of sin. Of course,
such blessings may come on Sunday evenings, too, or at
any other time, for that matter, when we seek the face of
God in worship.

(3). *Worship gives strength.*—Is there any better way
of beginning each week than in fellowship with God's

people in his house? In the natural course of events, the week will bring temptations and trials which require more than human strength to meet and surmount. The worship service can charge our spiritual batteries so that we go forth with God's help to meet the demands that await us. Through prayers and hymns and preaching we are reminded of the infinite resources that are ours in Christ. Knights of olden times were required to keep a night's vigil before God's altar as a preparation for their deeds of valor. We shall certainly prove, through attendance in God's house, that "they that wait upon the Lord shall renew their strength; they shall mount up with wings as eagles; they shall run, and not be weary; and they shall walk, and not faint" (Isa. 40:31).

(4). *Worship deepens fellowship.*—Even a great soul like Elijah cried, "I, even I only, am left" (1 Kings 19: 10). If we try to cultivate our religion in solitariness, we shall rob ourselves of one of life's greatest blessings and tend toward a pessimistic outlook, with a probable inclination to be critical of others. But to assemble on the Lord's Day with other children of God and to unite with them in his worship provides a stimulus which will enable us to be better Christians. To look over a crowded church auditorium and be able to say: "These, too, are God's children, and they are my friends," is to experience one of the deepest joys of Christian discipleship and church membership.

3. *Winning the Lost*

When, each returning Sunday, you make your way to church with your family, you are bearing a witness for God which he can use to the blessing of other lives. If you live a mile from the church, are you not preaching a sermon a mile long on the duty of acknowledging the claims of God? And if there is a smile on your face as you journey (as there most certainly should be), then you are telling others of the joys of serving the Lord.

It is eminently proper that our worship services should be occasions for presenting the gospel to the unsaved. Through the inspiration of the service they are made to feel the presence of God, and are thus prepared for the message from his Word which convicts of sin and points to the Saviour. Every Christian present contributes to the potential of blessing, and a company of praying people can create an atmosphere in which the miracle of the new birth can readily take place.

One of the greatest kindnesses we can render persons who are lost is to invite them to attend church with us. If we will sit with them, making them feel thoroughly at home in circumstances which may be somewhat unfamiliar to them, silently praying that God will speak to their hearts, there is a possibility that we will have the unspeakable joy of seeing them accept the Lord Jesus as Saviour.

If worship means to us all that is outlined in this chapter, then we shall be able to enter into the feelings of him who exclaimed: "I was glad when they said unto me, Let us go into the house of the Lord" (Psalm 122:1). Worship will be a recurring privilege and pleasure, to which we shall look forward from Sunday to Sunday and through which we shall find not only satisfactions for ourselves but also opportunities for service to others.

SUGGESTED TOPICS FOR DISCUSSION

1. Review the three principal elements in New Testament worship—prayer, praise, and preaching—and discuss the worshiper's share in each.

2. What aids do twentieth-century Christians have to an appreciation of the greatness of God?

3. How may Psalm 73:16–17 be repeated in the experience of the Christian worshiper?

OUTLINE

I. THE MEANING OF WORSHIP

1. The Broken Contact
2. A God-shaped Vacuum
3. The Answer of Revelation
4. The Response of Grateful Hearts

II. THE MANNER OF WORSHIP

1. A Place Provided
2. A Time Appointed
3. A Method Prescribed
   (1) The Old Testament superseded
   (2) "In spirit and in truth"
   (3) Prayer, praise, and preaching
   (4) A service of memorial

III. THE MINISTRY OF WORSHIP

1. Giving Glory to God
2. Enriching the Worshiper
   (1) Worship emphasizes reality
   (2) Worship brings understanding
   (3) Worship gives strength
   (4) Worship deepens fellowship
3. Winning the Lost

CHAPTER 5

Joy in Fellowship

JOHN WESLEY SAID that man was not meant to go to heaven alone. Just as the Jewish pilgrims traveled to Jerusalem in companies, so Christians are banded together that they may find mutual encouragement and help in their journey toward their eternal home. God means for us to find in our churches a fellowship which surpasses all others. Its keynote should be love, for did not Jesus himself say, "A new commandment I give unto you, That ye love one another; as I have loved you, that ye also love one another. By this shall all men know that ye are my disciples, if ye have love one to another"? (John 13:34–35).

The story is told of the apostle John, who recorded these words of Jesus, that when he tarried at Ephesus to extreme old age, and could only with difficulty be carried to church in the arms of his disciples, and was unable to give utterance to many words, he used to say no more at their several meetings than this: "Little children, love one another." The disciples and fathers who were there, wearied with hearing always the same words, said, "Master, why dost thou always say this?" "It is the Lord's command," was his worthy reply, "and if only this be done, it is enough."

Even when Jesus was with them, the twelve sometimes fell to disputing among themselves, and Paul had to reprove Christians who were divided by disagreement. So perhaps it is not surprising that discord occasionally mars the fellowship of a church in our day. It is not excusable that such things should happen, however, and we should certainly not allow the failures of a few to obscure the indisputable truth that there are no friendships in all the world to compare with those with which God's people are blessed.

I. THE EXAMPLE OF THE EARLY CHURCH

In his great study *The Church and the Ministry in the Early Centuries,* T. M. Lindsay indicates five outstanding elements in the New Testament conception of the church, the first of which was fellowship (*koinonia*). "This thought of fellowship," he says, "was the ruling idea in all Christian organization. All Christians within one community were to live in fellowship with each other; different Christian communities were to have a common fellowship. Visible fellowship with each other, the outcome of the hidden fellowship with Jesus, was to be at once the leading characteristic of all Christians and the bond which united them to each other and separated them from the world lying outside." [1]

The description of conditions in the first New Testament church, given in Acts 2:41–47, indicates the various areas in which this fellowship was exercised, with the clear implication that if this fellowship was broken at any point it was incomplete. The church member of those days who was anywhere careless toward the common responsibility and privilege which he shared with other church members, broke the circle of fellowship for himself, missed the corresponding blessing, and deprived the rest of that contribution to the general well-being of the group which he alone could make. The same is true today. True joy in church membership, for ourselves and for others, can only be experienced by a fellowship that is complete, lacking none of those parts which God has or-

[1] T. M. Lindsay, *The Church and the Ministry in the Early Centuries* (London: Hodder and Stoughton, 1902), p. 9.

dained for the mutual satisfaction of his people, for the strength of their witness before the world, and for the glory of him who is Lord of the church.

It is important, therefore, that we study Luke's description of church fellowship, carefully noting each factor involved and checking our own lives to see whether we are fulfilling our obligations to the church. Such a study may reveal some inadequacy which is robbing us of the full enjoyment of church membership and depleting the total good of the church to which we belong.

1. *Fellowship in Experience*

The soundest basis for true fellowship is a common experience. The hardships and hazards of service life, for example, bind war veterans together in organizations for mutual help and community service. Though butchers, bakers, and candlestick makers in civilian life, they find a bond of unity in their years of duty in uniform.

That which unites Christians is their experience of salvation in Christ. They represent all walks of life—the rich, the poor; the educated, the illiterate; the professional man, the farmer, the artisan; the young, the old. Yet, in spite of their diversity, they enjoy a delightful fellowship because Christ is their Saviour and Lord. As Paul put it: "Ye are all the children of God by faith in Christ Jesus. For as many of you as have been baptized into Christ have put on Christ. There is neither Jew nor Greek, there is neither bond nor free, there is neither male nor female: for ye are all one in Christ Jesus" (Gal. 3:26–28).

The ground at the foot of the cross is level. We stand equal in need and equal in blessing. "All have sinned, and come short of the glory of God" (Rom. 3:23) are words which embrace us all in universal condemnation. None can escape their inclusive indictment. There may

be degrees of guilt, but none is innocent at the bar of
divine justice; and one sin is enough to make a man
"come short." Hence, murderer and mischief-maker alike
must confess their failure before God and seek his mercy.
To all who come repentantly the promise is equally
given: "Believe on the Lord Jesus Christ, and thou shalt
be saved" (Acts 16:31). So, as saved men and women, we
gladly acknowledge ourselves the objects of divine grace.
We may have come to Christ from various backgrounds,
but we have only one testimony: "Thou wast slain, and
hast redeemed us to God by thy blood out of every kindred, and tongue, and people, and nation" (Rev. 5:9).

2. *Fellowship in Obedience*

Of those converted on the day of Pentecost it is said:
"They that gladly received his word were baptized"
(Acts 2:41). This was another factor in their fellowship.
They believed on Jesus unto salvation, and then they
obeyed him in the waters of baptism. Their baptism did
not save them. It did, however, declare their salvation,
and it qualified them for membership in the church. We
have earlier said that it is inconceivable that Peter and
the other apostles would have admitted into church membership any who did not possess saving faith in Christ.
Is it not equally inconceivable that they would have
added to the church roll the name of one who refused
to confess Christ by the appointed sign and method—believer's baptism?

There are those who charge that to insist upon New
Testament baptism as a condition for church membership is to impose an unnecessary and arbitrary demand.
We cannot speak for Christian groups who do not share
our conviction concerning believer's baptism. But for a
Baptist church there is surely nothing unnecessary or
arbitrary in requiring of candidates for membership that

they comply with the practice of that church. Where
Baptists have grown slack in this matter (and at some
times and in some places they have grown slack), it has
been to their own undoing. They have lowered their
standard—nay, more, they have lowered Christ's standard.
They have lost their distinctives. They have departed
from New Testament norms. And they have paid the
price in weakness and decline.

A sure ground for fellowship among Baptists is their
obedience to the Lord by confessing him before men in
the way he has ordained. "One Lord, one faith, one
baptism" (Eph. 4:5). The much-abused word "sacra-
ment" furnishes an illustration, for the *sacramentum*
was the military oath required of a Roman legionary. By
that solemn act of dedication a man became a soldier,
worthy to march under the eagles of Rome. We may re-
ject the word for its unhappy connotations (what a pity
it is when perfectly good words are spoiled!), but we can
appreciate the idea. Baptism is for us what the oath is
to the soldier: it is the indispensable requirement for
identification with a New Testament church: it is a glorious factor in the practice and enjoyment of Christian fellowship.

3. *Fellowship in Learning*

Most of us look back upon school days and school
friendships with growing appreciation. So we may be
glad that, for the Christian, life is a continuing learning
experience. To join the church is, in fact, to enrol in the
school of Christ; and much of the real satisfaction of
membership is to be found in the attention we give to
opportunities for adding to our understanding of Christ
and his way of life.

Checking once more on the Scripture passage under
consideration, we find that the early believers "continued

stedfastly in the apostles' doctrine [teaching]" (Acts 2: 42). This was something distinct from worship. While there are no details of the course of instruction followed, we cannot be far wrong to think of it as including the study of the Old Testament, particularly as it foretold the coming and ministry of the Lord Jesus Christ; the story of Jesus himself, told by those who had been privileged to be his companions; the explanation of his teaching as given, for example, in the Sermon on the Mount; instruction in the practices and purpose of the church and in the requirements of membership; and guidance in the principles of Christian living.

How tragic it is when church members fail to appreciate the importance of this fellowship of learning within the church. The result is seen in church members who know little or nothing of the doctrines of their church, of the content of the Bible, of the imperatives of the Christian life, and of the obligations of service—members, in fact, who are liabilities rather than assets to the cause of Christ.

Southern Baptists have unique opportunities to enjoy the fellowship of learning. They are offered a program of Christian education which embraces all ages and needs. The Sunday school, the Training Union, The Woman's Missionary Union, the Brotherhood, and other agencies of the church and denomination afford a comprehensive curriculum as interesting as it is important. To take advantage of these facilities for growth in knowledge will enrich the mind, strengthen the character, bless the soul, and bring untold rewards in deepening fellowship with other Christians, realized at its best in service together for Christ and the church.

4. *Fellowship in Association*

Even in the apostolic church, life was not all work.

"They continued stedfastly in the apostles' doctrine and fellowship," we are told; there was learning to be done, but there was also the relaxation of social fellowship. It is perhaps not by accident that the two experiences of learning and fellowship are linked in this statement. It is a perfect combination, as millions are proving today. In the Sunday school class, an Adult union, the Woman's Missionary Society circle, and the Brotherhood meeting, all of them learning situations, conditions exist which make the most delightful fellowship possible. Church members who suppose that they can fulfil the requirements of membership by putting in an occasional attendance at a Sunday morning worship service do not know what they are missing.

5. *Fellowship in Worship*

"And in breaking of bread, and in prayers"—so Acts 2:42 concludes. There is a strong body of opinion that the phrase "breaking of bread" refers to the observance of the Lord's Supper on the part of these pentecostal converts to the Christian faith. What could deepen the sense of unity, for them or for us, more than mutual participation in that commemorative meal, initiated by our Lord himself, and intended to recall his undying love for man? The significance of the supper, and its values to the soul, are discussed in chapter 4; so we pass on to note the reference here to fellowship "in prayers."

These early Christians did not neglect prayer. They prayed individually and as families but they also recognized the duty and the privilege of assembling as a church to present their thanksgivings and make their wants known at the throne of heavenly grace. In that exercise they discovered rich satisfactions, not only through fellowship with God, but also through fellowship with one another.

It would not be too much to say that present-day church members who get the most from and give the most through their church affiliations are invariably loyal to the prayer meeting. Prayer meeting is guarded against all encroachments. It is a midweek spiritual oasis, a trysting place for God's people, and, as Hugh Stowell says,

> . . . a spot where spirits blend,
> Where friend holds fellowship with friend.

6. *Fellowship in Sharing*

Conditions prevailing among the first Christian believers made necessary the measures described in these words: "All that believed were together, and had all things common; and sold their possessions and goods, and parted them to all men, as every man had need" (Acts 2:44-45). For many of these church members, the confession of Christ had proved costly. The apostles themselves were without economic support. As David Smith points out: "They had forsaken their homes and employments in the far north; and how could they maintain themselves, strangers as they were, in a hard and unfriendly city, prosecuting the while their evangelical ministry?" [2]

The answer to this need was a voluntary pooling of resources on the part of the church membership in Jerusalem—a step which met the immediate crisis, and was entirely commendable, even though it had later to be abandoned. Is it surprising that the spirit of fellowship thrived in an atmosphere as generous and unselfish as this? The very spirit of Jesus himself was expressed in the action of people who were willing to forego their own property rights in order that other Christians might be housed, clothed, and fed.

---

[2] David Smith, *The Disciple's Commentary* (London: Hodder and Stoughton, 1932) , Vol. 4, p. 33.

Methods have changed, but the churches of Jesus Christ have never lost this spirit of mutual responsibility and sharing. A sense of true brotherhood exists among those who bear the name of Christian, ready to reveal itself in deeds of consideration and solicitude toward those in need, and recognizing no limits to unselfish giving when emergency really strikes.

7. *Fellowship in Enjoyment*

The happiness of these first Christians is something we cannot overlook. Having received the gospel with joy (Acts 2:41) they continued to display a spirit of overflowing contentment in the togetherness of worship and social activity. "They, continuing daily with one accord in the temple, and breaking bread from house to house, did eat their meat with gladness and singleness of heart, praising God, and having favour with all the people" (Acts 2:46–47).

It is a poor advertisement for Christianity when professing Christian people seek their companionships and pleasures outside the church and its fellowship. What use is it to sing, with John Newton,

> Solid joys and lasting treasure
> None but Zion's children know,

and then to fill our week with a giddy round of worldly activity which loudly declares that there are deep voids in our hearts which religion has failed to fill?

Most of us need to recapture a sense of the sufficiency of the spiritual. We have become so infected with the spirit of the world that we behave as though happiness depended upon the possession of material abundance. We have grievously overlooked and undervalued what Paul calls "the inheritance of the saints in light" (Col. 1:12), and instead of living in the constant felicity of the goodness and the grace of God, we are trying to quench the thirst of our souls at broken and empty cisterns.

There is abundance of joy in Christian living, joy which defies circumstances, joy which is independent of having or getting, joy which belongs more to heaven than to earth. And the way into the experience of this joy is through fellowship with Christ and his people.

8. *Fellowship in Witnessing*

Though this thought is developed later in the book, this brief study of the factors which made for Christian fellowship in the New Testament church cannot be completed without noticing the concluding clause in Acts 2: "And the Lord added to the church daily such as should be saved." There is an obvious connection between the conditions in the church, as described in the earlier verses, and this statement of continuing growth.

A church at harmony within itself, composed of members to whom Christian fellowship is life's richest endowment, is a church whose very spirit witnesses to others and whose witness is inevitably effective. Moreover, the opportunity for witness constitutes the crowning joy of such a church fellowship, and the gladdest moment of each returning Lord's Day is when men, women, and children present themselves for membership upon profession of faith in the crucified and risen Lord. For the fellowship of the church is never exhausted in its outreach, and the more it embraces the richer it becomes.

II. FRIENDSHIP'S FINEST SETTING

The setting for church fellowship which we have so far considered in this chapter takes us back to the first century and to an environment so far removed from our modern world that perhaps we need to interpret some of the things we have discussed in terms of contemporary conditions. This, of course, we have already done in part; but it will be helpful at this point to think more specifically how church membership touches and enriches every area of life today, as it did for Christ's followers nearly two thousand years ago. Moreover, we need to recognize how we, as church members, can most fully explore this happy fellowship, for the satisfaction both of ourselves and of others.

1. *Our Social Instincts Satisfied*

Constituted as we are, it is inevitable that every normal person will seek social fulfilment in the company of other people of similar age, interests, and tastes. Unfortunately, this natural urge is not always wisely exercised. Some educators, for example, have misgivings concerning the desirability of fraternities and sororities for certain school ages and situations. How this instinct can be misdirected is seen in the hoodlum gangs of many of our larger cities, which unite youth only to debase it and which divert its energies into habits and activities which undermine personal morality and menace the security of the community.

It is very different when boys and girls are won to faith in Christ and enlisted into the fellowship of his church. The circle of friendship which they thus enter is no less satisfying than any other; indeed, it may confidently be claimed that the church is friendship's finest setting. Here social aspirations may have legitimate fulfilment, exercised under the guidance of Christian principles and directed into channels of increasing potentiality for personal blessing and usefulness. The Intermediates in any church should be the pride and joy of the church. Certainly no group can so thrill the truly Christian heart; for, when our teen-agers find their companionships within the church community and their activities within the church program, the prospect for the future is excellent—for them, for their families, for the church, and for the land we love.

Neither is this fellowship of the church for adolescents alone. It offers its blessings to every age and condition. It does not necessarily exclude other associations which do not possess its own distinctive qualities. It is probably true that the good church member should seek contacts with non-Christians through civic clubs and other social organizations. But the church surpasses them all and should have priority above them all, the church member permitting no other loyalty to clash with or come between him and his duty toward the community of faith. In the final analysis, he will find life's deepest and most enduring rewards in that companionship of worship, learning, and service which his church provides.

2. *"Make Friends of God's Children"*

"He who would have friends must show himself friendly" is a word of wisdom which probably explains the complaint of some people that they find only coldness in this or that church. If the criticism can be truthfully directed against any church that it lacks friendliness, then that church needs a heart examination. A young country lad, visiting a large city church, returned week after week without receiving a greeting or a smile. At length, one of the ushers confided to him that the congregation consisted of "the cream of society." Promptly the young visitor replied, "I think you mean the ice cream."

It ought not to be necessary for any church to describe itself as "the friendly church" since this should be characteristic of all. But there are church members who occupy their favorite seat Sunday by Sunday, stiffly shake hands with the usher as they enter and the preacher as they leave, and make no effort toward establishing friendly relations with other worshipers.

Look around your church auditorium next Sunday morning and you will see the finest people in the world. Get to know them, and you will introduce yourself into a fellowship which has no parallel. After all, this is your right and privilege, for there are no degrees of membership in the church: every person, young or old, belongs at the heart of things.

3. *Finding a Life Partner*

Did you ever hear the church criticized as "a matrimonial agency"? What some would make a point of criticism is in reality a strong commendation for the fellowship of Christian people. Of course, to join a church merely in the hope of meeting "Miss Right" is scarcely a worthy motive; but, even so, the Lord may mercifully overlook an ulterior purpose and give an unexpected blessing. That young people should find their dates and ultimately their life partners in the church is no matter for apology. It is of the glory of the church that it provides opportunity for young people to meet under Christian auspices, to develop acquaintance in the safest of circumstances, to pledge their affection under the blessing of heaven, and to embark upon married life with the tremendous advantage of mutual faith and spiritual interest.

A condition which can handicap a full experience of the joys of church membership is when husband and wife are not united in matters of faith. It is deeply unfortunate when those who share life's experiences at every other point have to part company at the church doors. Many fine and noble people are facing such a situation, and doing much better than just getting by with it; but they would doubtless be the first to acknowledge that it is not the ideal. For husband and wife, church membership can only be at its best when both are members of and

actively serving the same church. This is advice given too
late for some. It needs to be strongly impressed upon our
Baptist youth.

No warning against the marriage of a Baptist with a
Roman Catholic can be too strong. The full case against
such marriages cannot be given here; but the danger is
sufficiently great for earnest counsel against it. For the
Roman Catholic party to such a marriage there can be
only one condition for the union, a condition dictated by
his church—the complete surrender of the spiritual rights
of the other party. Where the marriage shall be held, who
shall officiate, what shall be the religion of the children
of the union—these and other things are all decided in
advance, with every advantage yielded to the Romanist.
There is no basis for true spiritual comradeship here, but
a prospect of widening division which can be bridged
only by the submission of one of the contracting parties
to the other's point of view. For the Roman Catholic
this would mean excommunication from his church. For
the Baptist (or any other non-Romanist) it would involve
the abandonment of conviction and surrender to a pitiless
ecclesiastical tyranny. How much better to avoid the
heartbreak and tragedy by marrying within one's own
faith and within the fellowship of one's own church!

4. *Families in Fellowship*

The joys of church membership are experienced at
their highest and best when families are united by the
ties of a like faith, attending church together, taking
their respective places in the program of the church, and
hallowing all home relationships in family worship.
There are few sights more delightful than to see father,
mother, and children arrive together at the church door,
going to their various places in Sunday school or Training
Union, and reassembling later that they may share in the

blessings of the worship service. And there are no families happier than those of whom this is true.

The program of Southern Baptists has the Christian family as its ideal and objective. Through the Cradle Roll earnest attempt is made to enlist not only babies, but also their parents, in the fellowship of the church. Sunday school and Training Union alike minister to all age levels, so that families may share together in every activity and each member may help the others in spiritual interest and growth.

Because of the intense desirability of spiritual unity within the family, children will pray for their unsaved parents and parents for their unsaved children. For the church as a whole, the first area of effort in evangelism should be the families of those already in membership. Not only is there the advantage of existing contact here, but the gaining of the objective, namely, the conversion of complete families, would bring the richest return for the church itself and for the cause of Christ as a whole. Well may we pray, in the words of the hymn, "God give us Christian homes."

III. "IN TROUBLE AND IN JOY"

As in the first century, so now, Christian fellowship finds its greatest opportunities for expression in times of crisis. Paul, in his exhortation to the Roman believers, wrote: "Rejoice with them that do rejoice, and weep with them that weep" (Rom. 12:15). If the Acts of the Apostles had then been written, he might have referred them to the record of their predecessors in the faith for examples. We who have the advantage of surveying the life of the church through the full sweep of the Christian centuries do not lack for evidence that there is no community of sympathy which can compare with the Lord's people.

1. *Sharing Life's Happinesses*

The common experiences of life afford continual opportunity to the church to demonstrate the depth of fellowship which exists among its members and to strengthen the ties which bind each to each and all to the Lord. This should include, of course, the joys as well as the sorrows which visit the membership. The birth of a child, for example—an event of unsurpassed delight within the circle of the family—should be made an occasion for rejoicing throughout the church. Much depends here upon the pastor, and he will be the first to recognize the importance and value of marking in some special way the joy which has come to a church family through the gift of a new life. Baptists, veering away as far as possible from any semblance of "infant baptism," have sometimes been remiss in failing to give recognition to an occurrence within the Christian fellowship which certainly calls for thanksgiving to God and also for congratulation to the family concerned. The least that might be done is an announcement of the birth in the church's weekly bulletin; and sanctified ingenuity can surely devise other means which, while giving due regard to Baptist convictions, may serve to indicate and express that happiness which a Christian group feels toward those of its number whom God has specially blessed.

A marriage within the church fellowship should be the occasion of rejoicing throughout the widest possible circle. Pastors are sometimes called upon to conduct wedding ceremonies for which they have qualified enthusiasm and toward which it may be difficult to show more than a casual interest. But how different when the couple standing before them are children of the church! Instead of looking round upon the faces of strangers, the officiating pastor sees mostly those whom he knows and loves, and, at the center of all, a young couple who, having grown up through Sunday school and Training Union and having met and courted in the happy atmosphere of the church's life, are now linking their destinies in the establishment of a Christian home. Such marriages are made in heaven.

It seems to be the pleasant lot of some churches to major on marriages of this kind. Of course, in these days, when young people travel far and wide, it is inevitable that some should form attachments with those who are not of their faith. But when Christian marriage is magnified in the home church, when young people grow up recognizing the joy which comes to a Christian fellowship as a whole when its members marry in the Lord, strong safeguards are furnished against unwise alliances, and lives are linked in prospect of mutual happiness and blessing.

2. *Solace When Sorrow Strikes*

Probably the values of Christian fellowship are never fully appreciated until, in some sorrow, we prove the strength and the tenderness of the ties which unite us. A Baptist family, moving a long way from its normal place of residence and its kin, was suddenly bereaved. Distance made it impossible for the members of this family to receive the comforts of their own relatives. But what they lacked in this way, through unavoidable circumstances, was made up to them through the demonstrated sympathy of the church to which they had so recently transferred their membership. Their home was transformed with floral gifts which declared the love and understanding of their fellow church members. "We did not know we were so rich in friends," these sorrowing hearts confessed.

The joys of church membership can be compensating joys, experienced in times of sickness, of anxiety, or of

loss. Each of us has opportunity to discharge a ministry
of sympathy and solicitude, and by our actions to enrich
the fellowship of the church to which we belong. A "get-
well" card, a telephoned inquiry, a letter of condolence,
or even a friendly handshake and smile may say to some
fellow Christian: "I am with you in this. The whole
church is with you. We shall not fail to pray for you. So
long as your trial lasts, we want to share it with you. When
it ends (as God grant it soon may), we shall share in your
rejoicing."

3. *"Bear Ye One Another's Burdens"*

We have seen how the church in Jerusalem helped its
own needy membership by a program of mutual sharing.
The time came, however, when disaster of such magni-
tude overtook this Christian community that it could not
help itself any longer. Famine, following upon persecution, threatened the very survival of the church—a situation which, when it became known among the Gentile
churches, was answered with abounding generosity. The
Fund for the Relief of the Jerusalem Believers was spon-
sored by Paul himself, who, acknowledging the generosity of the church in Philippi, wrote:

"We desire to let you know of the grace of God which
has been bestowed on the Churches of Macedonia; how,
amid a trial of great affliction, their abundant joy even in
their deep poverty has overflowed in the wealth of their
liberality. I testify that to the extent of their power, and
even beyond their power, they have of their own choice
given help. With earnest entreaty they begged from us
the favour of sharing in this service to the saints. They
indeed exceeded our expectations" (2 Cor. 8:1–5 Weymouth).

The Philippians knew the meaning of joy in fellowship. For them it was the joy of giving, now to their fellow

believers in Jerusalem, at other times to supply the needs of Paul himself. And Christian hearts continue to find joy in ministering to one another. Most churches have their love fund, or fellowship fund, contributed by members and used at the discretion of the pastor or of a committee to relieve cases of known distress within the membership. (Inquire into the policy, administration, and financial condition of this fund in your church.)

Calls for help received from deserving sources outside the immediate membership of our churches invariably receive generous response. "As we have therefore opportunity," wrote Paul to the Galatians, "let us do good unto all men," carefully adding, "especially unto them who are of the household of faith" (Gal. 6:10). "There are duties," says Calvin, commenting on this verse, "which we owe to all men arising out of a common nature; but the tie of a more sacred relationship, established by God himself, binds us to believers." It is that tie which creates the precious fellowship of the church in the practice and the realization of which our hearts overflow with joy.

SUGGESTED TOPICS FOR DISCUSSION

1. Discuss the place of the prayer meeting in enabling Christians to realize the joys of church membership.

2. How does the church contribute toward happy and successful marriage?

3. Review the provisions in your own church for assisting members in trial and misfortune.

OUTLINE

1. THE EXAMPLE OF THE EARLY CHURCH

  1. Fellowship in Experience

  2. Fellowship in Obedience

  3. Fellowship in Learning

  4. Fellowship in Association

  5. Fellowship in Worship

  6. Fellowship in Sharing

  7. Fellowship in Enjoyment

  8. Fellowship in Witnessing

II. FRIENDSHIP'S FINEST SETTING

  1. Our Social Instincts Satisfied

  2. "Make Friends of God's Children"

  3. Finding a Life Partner

  4. Families in Fellowship

III. "IN TROUBLE AND IN JOY"

  1. Sharing Life's Happinesses

  2. Solace when Sorrow Strikes

  3. "Bear Ye One Another's Burdens"

CHAPTER 6

Joy in Serving

IT WAS Jesus himself who said, "I am among you as he that serveth" (Luke 22 : 27). By his self-denying solicitude for others he dignified the idea of service and provided a pattern for his disciples to follow. The twelve were inclined to think of their association with Jesus in terms of advantage and reward; but by the example of his life and death he taught them that when we serve others we never step down but always step up.

The world has been blessed by those who have learned this lesson. The story of their contribution to humanity's welfare is written in the annals of our hospitals, the provisions of education, the humanitarianism of our laws, the achievements of our great philanthropic agencies, and in every effort to bring relief to the suffering, advantage to the underprivileged, and peace to this troubled world. Not all who have thus benefited mankind have borne the Christian name; but, knowingly or not, they have demonstrated the Christian spirit, and all men are their debtors.

The greatest service of all, however, is that which is consciously offered in Christ's name, and the greatest agency for this service is his church. But not all who belong to the church have made this discovery. If they had, they would enlist their lives with splendid abandon in service with the church, and the world would be transformed by their consecrated endeavors. Moreover, they would discover a consuming purpose in life which would be equally transforming for them. Millions of people are missing life's best merely for want of a guiding purpose. This should never be true of the Christian.

I. THE CHURCH: GOD'S CHANNEL OF BLESSING

1. *A World in Need*

One of the tenderest verses in the Bible describes the response of our Lord to the needs of men: "When he saw the multitudes, he was moved with compassion on them, because they fainted, and were scattered abroad, as sheep having no shepherd" (Matt. 9:36). His great heart was touched by the sight of physical suffering causing him to heal the sick and feed the hungry. But the depths of his nature were stirred by the knowledge of man's spiritual destitution, a knowledge which summoned him from heaven to earth. "For," says Paul, "ye know the grace of our Lord Jesus Christ, that, though he was rich, yet for your sakes he became poor, that ye through his poverty might be rich" (2 Cor. 8:9).

We cannot be touched with any true feeling of compassion for men until we have seen them through the eyes of Jesus. But it is of God's mercy that, at our fullest vision, we see only an infinitesimal part of what he sees. To have heaven's viewpoint of humanity in its total condition of physical misery, mental affliction, and spiritual plight would rob us of all peace of mind. The starving millions of India, the unnumbered blind beggars of the Orient, the misery of heathendom's child brides, the forgotten inhabitants of the world's jails, the toiling masses in Siberia's salt mines, the pitiful loneliness of the insane—this is only the beginning of the story. And God sees not only this but the moral bankruptcy and spiritual tragedy of mankind as well. Only his eye can survey all the dens of evil in which men hatch their hideous crimes, the palaces and hovels in which immorality hides itself, and the counsel rooms where tyrants plot the enslavement of nations. Only God knows the full remorse of the unregenerate dead.

It was because God saw everything that he acted in grace for the salvation of men. "He saw that there was no man, and wondered that there was no intercessor: therefore his arm brought salvation unto him; and his righteousness, it sustained him" (Isa. 59:16). The glory of the Bible message is that it is concerned not only with a God who created men but with one who has redeemed them as well.

2. *Redemption Through Christ*

Nothing in all of the gospel is more wonderful than the fact that Christ was the appointed Saviour of men from before the creation of the world (Rev. 13:8; Eph. 1:4). God planned the earth and peopled it in the knowledge that by so doing he was anticipating the time when he would have to send his own Son to the cross to reclaim his creation out of the hands of the devil. And Christ himself, described again and again as the agent of creation (John 1:3; Col. 1:16), put his hand to the making of men knowing that the same hand would one day be pierced to redeem them. Well might John exclaim: "Herein is love, not that we loved God, but that he loved us, and sent his Son to be the propitiation for our sins" (1 John 4:10).

If there is one thing we need to recover as Christians, it is a capacity for wonder. The gospel has lost its power over us and through us because it has become a commonplace in our thinking. The story is told of Robert Moffat, father-in-law of David Livingstone, that after he had translated the Fourth Gospel into the Chwana dialect of Africa, he took a copy of this gospel and began to read from it to a warrior of that tribe. The verse he read was

John 3:16, and the natives listened with amazed attention. When the missionary finished the verse, the warrior
cried, "Read that again!" Three times Robert Moffat read
the familiar words to this man. At length, flinging his
arms above his head, the African exclaimed: "Oh, that is
great news! Our gods do not love!"

"God so loved the world, that he gave his only begotten
Son." We have heard the words until they make little
impression on us. But they contain the most startling
news that the ears of men ever heard. They should be
engraven upon every redeemed heart. They should be
sounded abroad by every regenerate tongue. God loves us!
Christ died for us! There is forgiveness for every repent-
ant sinner! Death and hell are defeated! Heaven's gates
are opened wide! No wonder Paul described such news
as "the glorious gospel of the blessed God" (1 Tim. 1:11).

3. *The Commission of the Churches*

Christ established his church to be the channel through
which this message of abundant salvation might be delivered to men. There are some who erroneously suppose
that the church was a sort of afterthought in the mind of
God—an accommodation of his plans made necessary by
the success of his adversary, the devil. But the Scriptures
do not so teach. It was to church members that Paul
wrote: "God hath *from the beginning* chosen you to
salvation through sanctification of the Spirit and belief of
the truth: whereunto he called you by our gospel, to the
obtaining of the glory of our Lord Jesus Christ" (2 Thess.
2:13–14). Also, in a context rich in teaching concerning
the church, Paul describes the mission of the church as
"according to *the eternal purpose* which he [God] purposed in Christ Jesus our Lord" (Eph. 3:11).

Is this deep teaching? It is not so deep that the youngest
church member cannot grasp the glory of it. As church

members we belong to an institution which is—and has always been—at the heart of the divine program for the blessing of the world. Can any of the joys of church membership surpass this? By God's grace we have been brought into line with his eternal plan of redemption, and when we hear Jesus say (as he says to all who call him Saviour), "Go ye into all the world, and preach the gospel to every creature" (Mark 16:15), he is repeating for our benefit and obedience what God has been purposing for us down the long centuries of human existence.

II. SERVING WITHIN THE CHURCH

1. *Where Service Begins*

Within the field of Christian thinking there are a variety of opinions as to the New Testament meaning of the word church (*ekklesia*). Baptists have always emphasized the idea of the church as a local assembly of believers, but have usually been willing to recognize possible wider application of the word in such passages as Ephesians 1:22; 3:21; 5:23–29; and Colossians 1:24. There is apparent danger, however, in vague talk about the "universal church" when this diverts attention away from the fact that the individual believer can render effective service only through *a* church, that is, his own church, in which he places his membership. Is it not worse than useless to use ecstatic language about Christ's glorious church unless one's loyalty is demonstrated through devoted service to one particular church? There is a Spanish proverb which says that a bird may fly to the ends of the earth, but only in a nest can it raise a family.

The cause of the gospel has depended from the beginning upon consecrated lives functioning through church membership and finding their strength in co-operative service with their fellow members. The witness of the church in Jerusalem was discharged in this way. The missionary responsibility of the church in Antioch found expression in similar fashion. The splendid stewardship of the church in Philippi depended also upon the contributions of its various members. And the church on whose roll your name appears will only fulfil its true destiny in the plan and purpose of God as you and your fellow members give to it the utmost in love, loyalty, and effort.

2. *The Shame of Unemployment*

A joint conference of Southern Baptist agencies, meeting to discuss the nonresident member problem in our churches, passed a resolution which contains the following statements:

"Our churches face another problem equally as serious as the nonresident problem. This is the matter of enlistment of our resident church members and our fast growing number of recruits for membership. Last year this number was approximately 800,000. Next year it will probably go to a million. At present, at least 25 per cent of our resident church members are inactive. What we mean by 'inactive' is that they do not attend church except on rare occasions, that they do not contribute to the church's financial program, they are not enrolled in any of the organizations of the church, and they do not bear witness to Christ. The total church membership reported in the *Southern Baptist Handbook* for 1954 is 7,886,016. Subtract from that number 2,460,437 nonresident members, and we have a total resident membership of 5,425,579. We are certain that 25 per cent of the resident membership is completely inactive, as stated above. If this estimate is correct, and we believe it is conservative, there are 1,356,395 resident members who are just as much lost to service for Christ as if they were nonresident members."

These are alarming and shameful facts. Suppose we

look at them in terms of a church of 500 men[...] this number, taking the average for the denomina[...] whole, 156 would be nonresident, giving a re[...]nt church membership of 344. But 25 per cent of these are inactive, which means that the work of the church is being carried forward by 258 members, with 86 others content to do nothing.

The tragedy and the disgrace of such a condition could be expressed in many ways. Since our present study is concerned with joy in church membership, we must look at it in terms of what these inactive Baptists are losing through their failure to recognize and fulfil their sacred obligations. Like the third servant in our Lord's parable, they have kept their pound hidden in a napkin, that is, they have done nothing about their entrustment with the gospel. For such there awaits the stern rebuke of the Lord himself, "Out of thine own mouth will I judge thee, thou wicked servant," with the added verdict, "Unto every one which hath shall be given; and from him that hath not, even that he hath shall be taken away from him" (Luke 19:22, 26).

What is the condition of your church in the light of these statistics? Perhaps it is better than average. If so, this is something for which to be grateful. But we shall find no cause for complacency. Is it not true that the greatest anomaly in the kingdom of God is an inactive church member? So long as a single member in the fellowship of a particular church can be designated inactive, we have reason for self-examination as to why it is possible for people to align themselves with the church in apparent ignorance of what is required of them. The joy of the membership as a whole must be qualified and incomplete so long as any portion of that membership fails in its duty. For Paul has said: "Whether one member suffer, all the members suffer with it; or one member be honoured, all the members rejoice with it. Now ye are the body of Christ, and members in particular" (1 Cor. 12:26–27).

3. *A Place of Service for All*

A Southern Baptist church offers opportunity for happy service in Christ's name to all of its membership. The various departments of the church are organized with this end in view. None need lack some personal, specific task to discharge, for, apart from innumerable offices to fill in the programs of Sunday school, Training Union, Woman's Missionary Union, and Brotherhood, the unfolding year presents opportunity after opportunity to the willing heart.

The idea of personal service in the church begins in the children's departments of the various agencies where young Christians are enlisted for responsibilities which they may regard as their very own. The Training Union plays an important part in this project as it seeks to lead boys and girls, and young people and adults, into a fuller understanding of the church's ministry and a more effective participation in all of its program.

The contribution of Christian stewardship to the progress of the gospel is discussed in the next chapter. But it is impossible to proceed without mentioning the service which every member can render through giving. Though money ought never to be offered as a substitute for personal service, it does represent a means by which every Christian can take his share in the general work and witness of the church.

III. SERVING THROUGH THE CHURCH

1. *Church-Sponsored Evangelism*

If one outstanding explanation is sought for the fact that Southern Baptists are the fastest growing denomination in America today, we must point to the prominence given to evangelism in all of our church activities. The responsibility for winning others to Christ is not restricted to the pastor or the church staff. It is recognized as a responsibility equally shared by the entire membership and only discharged as every member takes his place in the evangelistic program of the church.

There are many methods for enlisting church members in the exalted task of soul-winning. In some churches extensive use is made of prospect cards. As the names of new residents in the community are obtained, cards giving all available particulars are made out, classified according to sex and age, and then distributed through Sunday school classes and units of the Training Union. Christians are thus challenged with the opportunity of visiting unsaved persons or unaffiliated Baptists, conversing with them in their homes, seeking to secure their attendance at church, eventually linking them in active fellowship for Christ.

The religious census presents another glorious opportunity for individual participation in soul-saving endeavor. By systematic visitation from house to house throughout a given area, every resident can be reached and records taken which will show the correct address, sex, age, church affiliation or preference, and other valuable particulars. It is not too much to claim that the religious census is the first step toward any program of enlargement within the church, and its results can furnish both the incentive and the material for intensive evangelistic efforts such as revivals.

Those who have never shared in visitation efforts may have a natural reticence toward them. But thousands who have at first said, "Me? I could never do that kind of thing!" have afterward discovered not only that they can do it but that it contains a thrill for them never before experienced. It is written of the seventy disciples, whom Jesus sent out two by two, that they "returned again with joy" (Luke 10:17). They had discovered the deep satisfactions of being about the Master's business as we may today when we serve him through the program of our church.

2. *Pioneering New Churches*

Is there any event in the home which brings more happiness than the birth of a child? This is a gladness in which every member of the family shares—brothers and sisters, father and mother, uncles and aunts, and grandparents in particular. So it is in the life of the church when, through the establishment of missions, new churches are developed. The heart of the true pastor rejoices to see the cause of Christ advanced, even though it be at the cost of losing some of his best workers. Do not parents have to part with sons and daughters that new homes may be begun? So God has ordained that churches shall multiply through the effort and the sacrifice of other churches—an effort and a sacrifice which have abundant compensations in overweights of joy.

There should be no such thing as a childless church. Wherever there are people, in town or in country, there is opportunity for a new witness in Christ's name; and the church which fails to propagate itself disappoints the Lord who died for it, deprives its community of a needed testimony, and robs its membership of an experience which can bring unparalleled rewards. The church with one or more missions provides training opportunities in Christian service for its members which will produce the pastors, educational directors, ministers of music, and missionaries of the future. It learns in actual experience that what is true for the individual is true also for the fellowship, namely, that the way to know real joy is to put

> **J**esus first
> **O**thers next
> **Y**ourself last

3. *For the Community's Good*

The Master who spoke of his followers as *salt* and as *light* (Matt. 5:13–16) clearly intended that their influence should be felt in the communities to which they belonged. Did he not offer the example of his own ministry which, while directed toward great spiritual objectives, nevertheless catered to humanity in its physical need? It is surely significant that the record of the pentecostal church in fellowship (Acts 2) is immediately followed by the healing of the lame man at the Beautiful Gate of the Temple. The joy of the man who was healed is made very plain for he "entered with them into the temple, walking, and leaping, and praising God" (Acts 3:8). But what of the joy of Peter and John who could say, "By the name of Jesus Christ of Nazareth, whom ye crucified, whom God raised from the dead, even by him doth this man stand here before you whole"? (Acts 4:10).

The church and the church member are not alone in rendering service to the community. Many who make slight profession of religion respond to the call of philanthropy. But the church and the church member are alone in this: that whatever they do, whether it be through hospitals for the sick or homes for the orphaned or food and clothing for the poor, is done for Christ and in Christ's name. This constitutes their special joy that in relieving pain and suffering they are directing the thoughts of men to the God of all grace and to his Son who said, in one of his most quoted utterances:

"Come unto me, all ye that labour and are heavy laden, and I will give you rest" (Matt. 11:28).

When the church member casts his vote for a good political candidate—and he should!—he acts in his Master's name. When he raises his voice against such evils as the liquor traffic—and he should!—he speaks his Master's protest. When he takes office in the community on a platform of Christian principles—and he should!—he represents his Master's way. When he fights prejudice and intolerance in any form—and he should!—he treads in his Master's footsteps. And for him this is joy, part of the unique joy of the church member. "Let *your* light so shine before men, that they may see your good works, and glorify your Father which is in heaven" (Matt. 5:16).

IV. THE SATISFACTIONS OF SERVICE

The happiest people are invariably busy people, and when our business is with the things of God, we experience a happiness which excels. We can see this illustrated in the life of Jesus himself. As a boy visiting the Temple, he apparently lost all sense of time, so engrossed was he in what he called "my Father's business" (Luke 2:49). Early in his public ministry, he surprised his disciples by his forgetfulness of his physical needs. "My meat," he said to them, "is to do the will of him that sent me" (John 4:34). In seeking to help the Samaritan woman whom he met at Sychar's well, our Lord lost all sense of hunger, and could therefore say, "I have meat to eat that ye know not of."

1. *Joy in Obedience*

A sure test of our love for the Lord is our willingness to obey him through service. For, although so many church members seem unaware of the fact, Christian service is a matter of obedience. When Jesus gave his commission to his disciples, he did not say, "I hope some of you will go into all the world and preach the gospel." He used the language of command, and said, "Go ye!" Neither did he wistfully ask, on the mount of ascension, that those he left behind would consider the possibility of being his witnesses. With the authority of a king he said, "Ye shall be witnesses unto me."

Think who this is who asks service from us! He is the One who left heaven's glory and accepted earth's poverty to reveal the Father to us. He is the One who went to the cross and died as the sinner's substitute. He is the risen Son of God, now sharing his Father's throne, and destined to rule universally. Could any honor surpass that of being in his employ? Could any joy be so great as to do his will?

Paul wrote, "I thank Christ Jesus our Lord, who hath enabled me, for that he counted me faithful, putting me into the ministry" (1 Tim. 1:12). His great heart was constantly thrilled by the thought that he held his appointment as a messenger of the gospel by direct assignment from his Lord. His last days, spent as a prisoner in Rome, with execution awaiting him, were brightened by the knowledge that he had done what the Lord had asked of him. Therefore he could write: "I have fought a good fight, I have finished my course, I have kept the faith: henceforth there is laid up for me a crown of righteousness, which the Lord, the righteous judge, shall give me at that day: and not to me only, but unto all them also that love his appearing" (2 Tim. 4:7–8).

There is joy in obedience for every child of God, and the words of Philip Doddridge should express the feelings of every redeemed heart:

> My gracious Lord, I own Thy right
> To every service I can pay,
> And call it my supreme delight
> To hear Thy dictates and obey.

2. *Gains in Personal Development*

Service for Christ invariably brings blessing through personal development. Every pastor knows what it is to observe the maturing of character and the increase of abilities which accompany the dedication of a life to the service of Christ and the church. To recall an actual example, there was George, who nearly fainted when someone who did not know his limitations called upon him for public prayer. George stammered and stuttered, and it was hard to know who was the more embarrassed—George himself or those who suffered for him, knowing how badly he felt. But the pastor found George a job to do—a class of Junior boys who needed teaching. Facing those boys Sunday after Sunday, George became more assured in his bearing and ceased to be afraid of the sound of his own voice. Before long, he was ready to stand to his feet whenever called upon. For many years afterward he proved himself a splendid teacher and a loyal deacon who could even take the pastor's place when need arose.

No department in the church renders more valuable help in this direction than the Training Union. There are hosts of men and women, occupying key positions in the kingdom of our Lord today, in all parts of the world, who began to qualify for such service through training received on Sunday evenings in their home churches. Theirs now is the joy of making a significant contribution to the cause of the gospel. When we are willing to place in Christ's hands the best that we have, it is amazing what skills he imparts and what opportunities he provides.

When we think of the material with which Jesus began when he called the twelve, and of the magnificent leadership which these same men rendered after the Lord had stamped the impress of his own character upon them, we cannot despair for ourselves. To each of us is given the opportunity of doing something worth while for God and humanity if we will begin with the task nearest to our hands, performing it with a sense of high privilege in the realization that we have been called into the service of the King.

3. *The Reward Ahead*

The Bible does not hesitate to speak of rewards for faithful service, and, as we have already seen, a Christian stalwart like Paul cheered his own heart in the emergency of impending violent death by the thought of the crown that awaited him. As the student works harder in contemplation of the diploma he will receive, and as the soldier strives more valiantly to gain another stripe, so the Christian is offered the promise of a heavenly prize.

The joys of Christian service can be experienced here and now. But they will be known at their highest and best when we hear the Master say: "Well done, thou good and faithful servant: . . . enter thou into the joy of thy lord" (Matt. 25:21). Heaven's joys will spring from earth's loyalties, but they will surpass our present joys as the sun outshines the flickering light of a candle. To know that in this life we have pleased our Lord will bring an eternity of satisfaction.

SUGGESTED TOPICS FOR DISCUSSION

1. Review the opportunities for Christian service offered in your church. Indicate areas where more workers are needed.

2. Describe and discuss the purpose and use of prospect cards.

3. What are the advantages gained by a parent church in the establishment of missions?

OUTLINE

I. THE CHURCH: GOD'S CHANNEL OF BLESSING

   1. A World in Need

   2. Redemption through Christ

   3. The Commission of the Churches

II. SERVING WITHIN THE CHURCH

   1. Where Service Begins

   2. The Shame of Unemployment

   3. A Place of Service for All

III. SERVING THROUGH THE CHURCH

   1. Church-sponsored Evangelism

   2. Pioneering New Churches

   3. For the Community's Good

IV. THE SATISFACTIONS OF SERVICE

   1. Joy in Obedience

   2. Gains in Personal Development

   3. The Reward Ahead

CHAPTER 7

Joy in Co-operating

WITH THE Holy Spirit as our instructor, even a visit to a zoo can teach us important lessons. In Proverbs 30 : 24–28, four of God's smallest creatures are presented as examples of wise behavior. The third of these is the locust, of which it is said: "The locusts have no king, yet go they forth all of them by bands." A solitary locust could easily develop an inferiority complex, so limited are his powers. But a swarm of locusts, as some parts of our own country have learned from painful experience, can be devastatingly destructive.

When people unite, either to do bad or to do good, their individual weaknesses and shortcomings are lost in the power of the group, a power which can become progressively strong until it is almost irresistible. History affords many examples such as the French Revolution. The underprivileged masses of France were powerless against their aristocratic oppressors until they became organized. Then, by the instrument of terror, they changed the political face of France, ending the monarchy and substituting the republic in its place. By more peaceful methods, labor has gained a voice in the councils of industry of most western countries through the formation of labor unions. The inaudible voice of the individual worker becomes articulate through an organization of millions which functions as his representative.

God's plan for his people is that they should worship and witness together as churches so that, through cooperative effort, great achievements might be possible in

his name. Since New Testament times this co-operation
has been exercised on various levels, beginning with the
individual church. Each new convert to faith in Christ
finds himself introduced to a community of faith, within
the church of his membership, which brings to him a satisfying sense of belonging and enables him, by united endeavor, to bring great things to pass. But, through his
church, this same person enters into a wider fellowship
by which he is identified, in service and testimony, with
an ever-increasing circle of men and women who share
both his experience, his convictions, and his aims. He discovers that he has linked his life with a spiritual movement of unsuspected proportions. He has joined a brotherhood which crosses frontiers of color, race, and language. In fact, he belongs to the biggest and noblest thing
in all the world.

I. SUPPORTING YOUR CHURCH

1. *In Its Program*

One of the first inquiries made of a candidate for missionary service concerns the quality of his church membership. A person who has failed to make his contribution
of effort to Christ's cause through his church is not likely
to make a successful worker elsewhere. Our duty toward
our Lord begins right where we are. He expects us to win
our spurs on local battlefields before he commissions us to
carry the standard of the gospel to outposts of kingdom
strategy. Did he not expressly say to his apostles, "Beginning at Jerusalem"? (Luke 24:47). Though he longed to
reach the last person in the world with the message of his
love, Jesus knew that the successful worker must start at
the center and work out to the circumference. The way
to touch the largest number of lives for Christ and reach
the farthest distance with his gospel is to put our best into

the program of our church, whether it be a one-room building in the country or a block-wide city edifice. This is the place to which God has appointed us, and here we can serve him best.

2. *In Its Business*

A modern church not only requires good organization but good administration as well. Because it is in business for God, it will seek efficiency in its affairs combined with economy in its expenditure. "Let all things be done decently and in order" (1 Cor. 14:40) might well be the motto of every New Testament church.

In some denominations, church business is the responsibility of officials or committees which function without reference to the membership. Baptist churches, however, accept the democratic principle that every member has a right to express himself on the business of the church, both articulately and by ballot. For this purpose, regular business sessions are held, and, when exceptional matters require urgent attention, emergency sessions are summoned.

The pity is that many church members never assume any administrative responsibility unless they happen to be at a meeting which is unexpectedly called into business session. Then they are probably so uninformed on the affairs under discussion that they are unable to make an intelligent contribution to the proceedings.

The church member who takes a genuine interest in his church will surely want to keep himself informed on everything that pertains to its work and witness. He will attend business meetings whenever possible, proving himself a good listener and a helpful participant when he has something constructive to say. He will welcome opportunities to serve on church committees. He will count it a high honor and a priceless privilege if he is elected to serve as a deacon. Because his church means much to him, he will derive increasing happiness from giving it the benefit of his experience and from sharing with other members in the responsibility of guiding its affairs wisely and well.

3. *In Its Budget*

We have so often said, "Money isn't everything," that perhaps we have tended to overlook how very important money is. The cause of the gospel is dependent upon money—not only upon money, it is true, but God has ordained that his work in this world shall go forward or lag behind according as his people give or withhold their substance. Moreover, the joys of church membership are in a great degree dependent upon an adequate steward-ship of possessions. Jesus himself said, "It is more blessed [happy] to give than to receive" (Acts 20:35).

Those who practice tithing (an ever-increasing num-ber in the membership of Southern Baptist churches) are unanimous in testifying to the spiritual blessing it has brought into their lives. The tither gives back to God a scriptural proportion of his income, not as a legal require-ment, but as a token of his love and gratitude to the Lord and as an expression of his recognized obligation toward others. Sunday by Sunday, as he places in the offering plate at least one tenth of what the Lord has given him, he rejoices in the privilege of serving God in this way. The thought of the many good causes that will be helped by his gift stimulates him to pray for all of the workers con-cerned, and he realizes that though he may never leave the shores of his native land, he is a missionary, both at home and abroad, through his money.

To bring our offerings to God in expectation of rec-ompense, as though the Lord ought to match every dollar with a dollar's worth of blessing, would be to degrade the

New Testament conception of Christian stewardship. Not blessings to come but blessings already received are the incentive of worthy giving. The saved person begins the Christian life with an indebtedness to God which he can never fully discharge. What can we offer God for the gift of his Son to be our Saviour? Surely Isaac Watts had the right idea when he wrote:

> Were the whole realm of nature mine,
>   That were a present far too small;
> Love so amazing, so divine,
>   Demands my soul, my life, my all.

But, such is the grace of God, though we give in acknowledgment of his past goodness and his present favor, he surprises us with added evidences of his love and care. The very act of giving fills our hearts with joy, and the more we give the more that joy increases. Our church membership becomes precious to us as we multiply our investment in the church. The cause of missions takes on new appeal and interest as we commit ourselves to it through our gifts. People who were but names before become active partners with us in gospel service as we contribute to their support by the offerings we bring. Our horizons broaden, our world becomes bigger, life assumes a significance hitherto unrealized when we dedicate to God an adequate proportion of that with which he blesses us. This is one of the indescribable joys of church membership.

II. WORKING WITH OTHER BAPTISTS

The Christian who follows the New Testament pattern in his church loyalty will soon discover that his membership has introduced him to a fellowship which is ever growing. Though the automony of each church is clearly indicated in the Acts of the Apostles and the epistles,

equally evident is the existence of a bond of union between the churches. The church in Antioch, for example,
when faced with a crisis which demanded wise handling,
referred its problem to the church in Jerusalem (Acts 15).
Later, when the Jerusalem church was afflicted by famine,
various churches contributed to a fund which brought relief to the stricken believers in Palestine. Paul, it may
also be noted, wrote at least two of his epistles (Galatians
and Ephesians) to groups of churches, a course made possible by the fellowship of church with church, so that the
sharing of these letters presented no difficulty.

1. *The Value of Associations*

This happy condition is projected into Baptist church
life by means of associations, usually city- or county-wide,
which bring the churches of a given locality together for
mutual encouragement and united endeavor. It has often
been claimed that the association is the key to denominational co-operation and progress. It would certainly be
difficult to promote the programs of Sunday school,
Training Union, Woman's Missionary Union, and Brotherhood if it were not for associational organizations, and
the mission boards would be seriously handicapped in the
presentation of their programs apart from the facilities
which the associations afford.

For the individual member, the association offers the
opportunity of getting to know other Baptists on the high
ground of service together in Christ's name. Some of the
great occasions of the year are associational rallies at
which churches, geographically grouped, get together to
hear reports of work accomplished, to project plans for
the future, and to share the inspiration of worshiping together as fellow Baptists. These meetings, held regularly
in the associations, provide information and inspiration
which greatly stimulate Christian activity.

2. *Your State Organization*

The division of our country into states set the inevitable pattern for Baptist organization. Each state in which Southern Baptists have sufficient representation has its own convention, or general association as it is sometimes called. These numbered twenty-three after the inclusion of Ohio in 1953. Many of the state conventions sponsor their own mission activities, designed to meet local conditions and needs, while the denominational programs of Sunday school, Training Union, Woman's Missionary Union, and Brotherhood are promoted through state offices, each department of work having its own staff.

An important service rendered at the state level is the publication of what are usually referred to as Baptist state papers—news journals, published weekly for the most part, which carry information on Baptist life and work in the respective states and on a Convention-wide basis, plus the story of missionary activity at home and overseas. Since one of the recipes for enjoying church membership is to be well-informed, it behooves every Southern Baptist to keep his interest stimulated by reading his state paper. If he can attend meetings organized at a state level —perhaps acting as messenger for his church at the annual state assembly—he will discover new satisfactions in his church membership as he realizes the numerical strength of the fellowship to which he belongs and learns more of its service for Christ and its spiritual potentials.

3. *The Southern Baptist Convention*

In 1845, the Southern Baptist Convention was organized, the purpose of which is stated as follows: "To provide a general organization for Baptists in the United States and its territories for the promotion of Christian missions at home and abroad and any other objects such as Christian education, benevolent enterprises, and social services which it may deem proper and advisable for the furtherance of the kingdom of God." The Convention itself functions directly only once a year, when messengers from co-operating churches assemble at an appointed place to receive the reports of denominational agencies and committees and to transact any necessary business. All issues are freely discussed under parliamentary rules, and each messenger present has an equal right to be heard. The claim has been made that the Convention demonstrates democratic principles at their best.

The Convention discharges its responsibilities and carries out its plans through its agencies—the Foreign Mission Board, the Home Mission Board, the Sunday School Board, the Relief and Annuity Board, its five seminaries (Southern Baptists have a joint interest in a sixth—the American Baptist Theological Seminary for Negroes), the Southern Baptist Hospital (New Orleans, Louisiana, with a branch at Jacksonville, Florida), the Southern Baptist Foundation, the Radio Commission, and the Southern Baptist Historical Commission. It also has three other commissions (Christian Life, Education, and Baptist Brotherhood) and two standing committees (Public Affairs and Order of Business). The Woman's Missionary Union is an auxiliary of the Convention. All of these interests are co-ordinated through the Convention's Executive Committee, with offices in Nashville, Tennessee, of which Dr. Porter Routh is executive secretary-treasurer. This committee carries on the work of the Convention when it is not in session.

So brief and inadequate a statement on the Southern Baptist Convention may not arouse much enthusiasm. But a few minutes of thought given to each of the agencies mentioned in the previous paragraph will surely stimulate the mental picture of a glorious, worldwide testimony for Jesus Christ. God has greatly blessed Southern Baptists and has placed before them an opportunity that has no parallel. At this critical period in the world's history, the possibility of significant service lies before them. They have the manpower, the organization, the program, and the financial resources to do exploits for Christ and his kingdom. How wonderful to be able to say: "I belong to this great fellowship of Baptist people, working together for humanity's highest good. I am part of this mighty instrument for gospel witness and Christlike service." Such a realization should induce humble gratitude and profound happiness.

4. *The Cooperative Program*

The Southern Baptist church member has the answer to the question, How may I best put my money to work for God? That answer is the Cooperative Program. Think of a person whose tithe is $100. If he had to make his own inquiries and calculations, he would find it very difficult to distribute his money among Baptist causes in proportion to their respective needs. Assembling facts, listening to appeals, weighing needs, evaluating opportunities—all this would be an impossible task for him. But it is a task which is done for him through the Cooperative Program.

He brings his tithe of $100 to his church. Decision has already been taken by the membership as to what proportion the church needs for its own work. If his church attains to the ideal, it will keep only half of the $100 for this purpose. The balance of $50 is turned over to the state organization which, in turn, withholds what is necessary for the maintenance of state missions, hospitals, schools, and so forth, and what remains is forwarded by the state to the executive secretary-treasurer of the Southern Baptist Convention, whose office is in Nashville, Tennessee. If a fifty-fifty division has been determined by the state, this means that $25 of the original $100 reaches Nashville to become part of a large fund which is distributed among the Southern Baptist Convention agencies.

By this means, the church member's tithe of $100 is used to support gospel work reaching from his home church to the furthermost point of the foreign mission field. Along the way, it helps to put some young person through a Baptist college, takes a part responsibility for the care of a patient in a Baptist hospital, contributes to the support of a worker among Negroes, and gives a helping hand to the state organization in all of its departments of work. Some proportion of the $100 will enable the gospel to be proclaimed on Indian reservations; another part will help to educate a young preacher in a Southern Baptist seminary; and yet another will befriend an orphan in a children's home.

Surely all of this represents an investment in happiness for both the giver and those who benefit from his giving. It indicates one of the privileges of church membership and challenges every Baptist to the utmost in stewardship that, by means of the Cooperative Program, every need of every agency may be met and the witness extended both in the homeland and on the far-flung fields of missionary endeavor.

III. IN SERVICE FOR THE WORLD

"Know your denomination" is excellent advice for the Baptist who wants to derive all of the values of inspiration, information, and co-operation from his church membership. Those whose horizons are bounded by the walls of their church and who know little or nothing of the nation-wide and worldwide activities carried on in the Southern Baptist name, deprive themselves of some high points of genuine pleasure. Some of these activities are described here.

1. *Evangelism in the Homeland*

Over thirty thousand churches, twenty-three state organizations, and the Home Mission Board share the responsibility for Southern Baptist witness in the United States itself. To think of these churches is to envisage a mighty work of evangelism which is touching every segment of our national life. The contribution of the rural church is being increasingly realized. It is strikingly illustrated by the large proportion of dedicated leadership which flows into the denomination—and into all spheres of our national life—from country churches. In towns and cities, too, our churches furnish the light which leads men to Christ and the salt which preserves the good and arrests the evil in these communities.

The varying programs of the state conventions, each adapted to meet local conditions and needs, cannot be described here. (It is suggested that the reader obtain information from his own state office.) Neither is it possible to do more than mention the worthy program of the Home Mission Board which provides missionaries to many racial groups including Indians, Chinese, Mexicans, French, and Jews, as well as to afflicted people such as the deaf. It also reaches out to territories like Alaska, Panama, the Canal Zone, and Cuba, establishing mission stations and assisting in the formation of churches. Every church member should keep abreast of these activities by reading *Home Missions,* the monthly magazine of the Home Mission Board.

2. *Varied Ministries in Christ's Name*

How easy it is to assume that the program we enjoy as Southern Baptists is similar to that of Baptists in other parts of the world. It would certainly contribute to our sense of gratitude and privilege if we could grasp the ex-

tent to which we possess advantages of which other Baptists know nothing. Take our schools and colleges, for
example. These are a source of surprise and amazement
to Baptists visiting us from other lands, who, in most cases,
have no denominational schools. Baptist hospitals are another provision practically unknown beyond America's
shores. These ministries of education and healing, carried
on in Christ's name, are a rich inheritance which we have
received from our pioneering fathers, each of them
prompting us to appreciation and thankfulness and adding to our responsibility.

A word seems appropriate here concerning the Sunday
School Board, with particular reference to its output of
religious literature. This board is unique in that it does
not depend upon the Cooperative Program for its support, but actually contributes from its earnings to many
phases of our denominational life. Its greatest service is
rendered direct to the churches through its promotional
activities and its vast distribution of published materials.
To give actual statistics is almost useless since today's
records are broken by tomorrow's. Giant printing presses
are kept busy day and night producing mountains of
Christian literature for Sunday school, Training Union,
and Baptist Student Union—magazines for the church
choir, for the home, for devotional guidance—and books
on a variety of subjects for readers of all ages. To think of
this ceaseless flow of publications, all Bible centered and
Christ glorifying, is to be thankful again for belonging.

3. *The Cause of Foreign Missions*

The world owes an incalculable debt to the English
Baptist, William Carey, through whose vision and per-
sistence modern missions were launched. It is with justi-
fiable pride that we claim spiritual kinship with such a
man. Perhaps we should not find equal reason for pride

in our own record of world evangelization. Southern Baptists have done much to spread the gospel. But, in the light of their greater resources, they have done less than others. The average church member gives under seven dollars annually to missions of all kinds, of which amount a little over one dollar goes to foreign missions. So long as such a condition continues, Mr. Average Member is short-changing himself; for apart from the blessing his money might bring to others, he is missing the joy of the good steward.

Those who give generously for mission causes, however —and they are many—can thank God for the privilege of supporting a group of men and women who belong to the aristocracy of heaven. In Latin America, Africa, Europe, the Near East, and the Orient a growing army of consecrated and talented workers are supported through the Foreign Mission Board. Whatever the inadequacies of the past, the future is bright with promise. Candidates of splendid caliber are coming forward as volunteers for overseas service. There is greater awareness among the churches of their responsibility as trustees of the gospel for the whole world. Gifts to foreign missions through the Cooperative Program are increasing, while the annual Lottie Moon Offering establishes new records from year to year, thanks to the devoted efforts of the Woman's Missionary Union.

The church member who reads *The Commission,* the monthly magazine of the Foreign Mission Board (and this, of course, should mean every church member) will continually thank God for the victories that are being gained in Christ's name in lands far and near. He will feed the flames of his own enthusiasm from the fires which burn in the hearts of the missionaries, and the thought that his own self-denials are helping to make their witness possible will surely take him often to his knees in prayer.

IV. LINKS WITH OTHER CHRISTIANS

1. *Oneness in Christ*

A great Christian of the past used to say, "If you love my Lord, give me your hand." This is a sentiment which Baptists can echo. Though tenaciously holding their distinctive doctrines, and though firmly believing that in their church order and practice they correctly interpret New Testament teaching, Baptists freely recognize the right of others to disagree with them and to follow the light as they see it. They acknowledge that the frontiers of God's kingdom lie beyond the lines which denominations have drawn, and they greet as brethren all who love the Lord in sincerity and who honor the authority of his Word.

2. *Levels of Co-operation*

Southern Baptists believe in co-operation at every point where this is possible without the surrender of principle. They have consistently declined to affiliate with movements which look in the direction of a united church, such as the National Council of Churches or the World Council of Churches, believing that the cause of Christ will not be served by the abandonment of denominational convictions. But they have eagerly joined hands with members of other Christian groups in order to present a solid front against moral and social evils or against threats to the spiritual freedom of our land. Baptists, for example, have taken a prominent part in antiliquor activities, in endeavors to preserve the separation of church and state, and in the work of the American Bible Society, conducted at an interdenominational level.

How this co-operation may be realized and expressed in community situations is something which must be worked out in the light of local conditions. The important thing is that we show love and understanding toward other Christian groups, and follow the leadership of the Holy Spirit in our quest for opportunities for mutual fellowship and service. The more we do this, the greater the enrichment of our own lives. We shall doubtless discover in other Christians spiritual qualities which will inspire us to deeper consecration and higher endeavor.

V. A WORLD FELLOWSHIP OF BAPTISTS

It is estimated that there are over twenty million Baptists throughout the world. The greater part of these are to be found on the American continent. There are groups of varying size in the countries of Europe. The Baptists of Australasia, though a minority among the denominations, are all the time growing in strength and achievement. In Africa, partly from immigration and partly from the work of missions, there is a considerable Baptist representation. And in every country into which Baptists have taken the gospel in obedience to the Great Commission, churches both large and small are to be found which follow the same pattern of New Testament practice and belief.

1. *The Baptist World Alliance*

As far back as 1790, a world fellowship of Baptists was proposed. Two centuries later, eminent Southern Baptists were discussing the same thing. This time something was done about it. When British Baptists were acquainted with the idea, they responded heartily, and an invitation was extended to the Baptists of the world to meet (by representation, of course) in London, in the summer of 1905. Thus the first session of the Baptist World Alliance was held, attended by nearly three thousand people, who adopted a constitution the preamble to which reads:

"Whereas, in the providence of God, the time has come when it seems fitting more fully to manifest the essential oneness in the Lord Jesus Christ as their God and Saviour, of the churches of the Baptist order and faith throughout the world, and to promote the spirit of fellowship, service, and co-operation among them, while recognizing the independence of each particular church and not assuming the functions of any existing organization, it is agreed to form a Baptist Alliance, extending to every part of the world."

At intervals of five years, except where war prevented, the Alliance has convened a Baptist World Congress, held in different countries as circumstances have permitted. The last congress to meet in the United States was in Cleveland, Ohio, in 1950. Five years later, in 1955, the choice was London once more, on which occasion a total registration of 8,600 was recorded.

2. *A United Voice*

Southern Baptists, who played a prominent part in the launching of the Baptist World Alliance, have continued through the years to give it their enthusiastic support. The individual church member, though probably never having the opportunity to attend a Baptist World Congress, can find gratification in the thought that, through the alliance, he and his church are linked with Baptists everywhere. When he hears of Baptist minorities being discriminated against, and even persecuted, by foreign governments, he may find happiness in the thought that the united voice of world Baptists (which, of course, includes his voice) is making itself heard on behalf of the victimized groups through the Baptist World Alliance.

3. *Benefiting One Another*

This fellowship on a worldwide scale brings its advantages to all concerned. Southern Baptists, for example, possess numerical and financial strength, and they major in evangelism. They have a contribution to make to Baptists in other lands. But many of the smaller groups have spiritual qualities with which they can enrich the lives of others. The very trials they have endured have given them a depth of conviction and a strength of testimony which all may emulate; and almost without exception they possess a capacity for reverence, expressing itself in dignified worship services, from which all may learn. In this happy fellowship of spiritual give and take all Baptists are helped, and the cause for which they stand is correspondingly strengthened.

What does this chapter teach us? That, as Baptists, we have opportunities for fellowship with other Baptists on a number of levels, beginning with our own church, on through association and state organizations to a glorious denominational fellowship through the Southern Baptist Convention, and finally attaining worldwide proportions in the Baptist World Alliance. To pursue this fellowship from level to level can be a most rewarding experience. But even those who, through force of circumstances, may never get further than the associational level in the enlargement of their contacts may realize with sincere thanksgiving to God that they are united in faith and service with a mighty host of men, women, and children who witness for Jesus Christ under the Baptist name.

SUGGESTED TOPICS FOR DISCUSSION

1. Contrast Baptist church administration with the methods of other denominations.
2. Review the three levels on which a Southern Baptist church may have fellowship with other churches of the same order.

3. In what ways does the Co-operative Program serve the church member in helping him to fulfil his financial stewardship? '

OUTLINE

I. SUPPORTING YOUR CHURCH

   1. In Its Program

   2. In Its Business

   3. In Its Budget

II. WORKING WITH OTHER BAPTISTS

   1. The Value of Associations

   2. Your State Organization

   3. The Southern Baptist Convention

   4. The Cooperative Program

III. IN SERVICE FOR THE WORLD

   1. Evangelism in the Homeland

   2. Varied Ministries in Christ's Name

   3. The Cause of Foreign Missions

IV. LINKS WITH OTHER CHRISTIANS

   1. Oneness in Christ

   2. Levels of Co-operation

V. A WORLD FELLOWSHIP OF BAPTISTS

   1. The Baptist World Alliance

   2. A United Voice

   3. Benefiting One Another

CHAPTER 8

Joy in Witnessing

THE JOYS of church membership do not depend ultimately upon others though they be our fellow members,
or upon church activities however well planned, or upon
a great denominational program. The joys of church
membership depend more than anything else upon the
quality of our own Christian experience and living.

God's intention for our happiness is clearly in evidence.
The world he has given us to live in abounds in provisions
for joys unspeakable. He could have made birds without
a song, flowers without a scent, trees without fruit, and
the sky without a sunset. But a loving Heavenly Father
has provided these and other adornments of his creative
skill that the hearts of men might be made glad and their
thoughts directed toward him. Moreover, his spiritual
provisions surpass all of his material blessings, justifying
the psalmist's exclamation: "Happy is that people, whose
God is the Lord" (Psalm 144:15).

Two things destroy the possibility of our happiness:
sin in the unregenerate and insincerity in the Christian.
It is with the second that we are now concerned. The
purpose of the Christian life is that we should be witnesses to the power of Jesus Christ (Acts 1:8), a witness
in this sense being not only a spectator but a testifier also.
A Christian should certainly be an observer of Christ's
power in his own life and the lives of others. But he becomes a witness only when he declares and demonstrates
that power. How imperative this is, Jesus himself made
plain when he said: "Whosoever therefore shall confess

me before men, him will I confess also before my Father
which is in heaven. But whosoever shall deny me before
men, him will I also deny before my Father which is in
heaven" (Matt. 10:32–33).

The extent to which we are witnesses for Jesus, as members of his church, will prove to be the measure of our
Christian joy. It is important, therefore, that we consider
ways and means by which we may bear this witness individually and jointly in the fellowship of the church.

I. WITNESSING BY PERSONAL LIFE

1. *By Our Experience of Salvation*

When Paul wrote to the Ephesians about "the whole
armour of God" (Eph. 6:13–17), he described a Roman
soldier in the process of putting on his military equip-
ment. Paul had many opportunities to watch this very
thing. Therefore he began where every Roman soldier
began: "First fastening round you the girdle of truth"
(v. 14 Weymouth). He was referring to a leather harness
to which the soldier fastened the other items of his pro-
tective gear. But, in his spiritual application, he was
emphasizing the necessity for a foundation of true, sincere, genuine faith. We sometimes speak of saving faith,
and that, surely, is what is meant here. Who could hope to
be a successful warrior for Christ unless his enlistment
met the requirements of his great Captain? Those requirements are repentance and faith.

In the same vein, Peter wrote: "Add to your *faith* virtue; and to virtue knowledge," and so on through a cata-
logue of Christian qualities (2 Peter 1:5). There could
be no Christian character, in Peter's understanding, that
did not begin with what he had previously called "precious faith" (v. 1). As the pieces of a Christian's armor
hang upon the belt of truth, so the edifice of Christian

character must be raised upon the foundation of faith.

It is good for us to retrace our steps to Calvary, and to live over again that "happy day, when Jesus washed our sins away." Ask yourself, Christian: What did he do for me there? Examine again the certificate of your heavenly adoption, signed in the blood of God's Son. To do so will chase your doubts away. It will restore your confidence. It will lighten your burdens. It will illumine your prospects. It will sharpen your testimony. Your witness depends, in fact, upon the assurance of your salvation.

2. *By the Proof of Regeneration*

"We were . . . we are . . ." wrote Paul to the Ephesian believers (2:5, 10), expounding a subject which was at the heart of his teaching, namely, the difference which Christ makes in the redeemed life. In those days, as now, church members were inclined to erase the clear line of separation which God draws between his children and the world. Converts, won from heathenism and continuing to live in their old environment, tended to take the easy way of conforming to the prevailing pattern rather than challenging that pattern by the contrasted integrity of their lives.

The baptized believer has no excuse for forgetting the Christian obligation to "walk in newness of life" (Rom. 6:4). The memory of his own baptism, and every baptismal service he observes, confronts him with the parable of the liquid grave: "If we have been planted together in the likeness of his death, we shall be also in the likeness of his resurrection" (Rom. 6:5). This is a truth with an immediate application, as the same apostle indicated to another church when he wrote: "If ye then be risen with Christ, seek those things which are above, where Christ sitteth on the right hand of God. Set your affection on things above, not on things on the earth. For ye are dead, and your life is hid with Christ in God" (Col. 3:1–3). To make his meaning absolutely plain, Paul proceeded to list some forbidden things for the Christian which must be thrust aside so that "kindness, humbleness of mind, meekness, longsuffering" and other Christlike qualities may be displayed.

3. The Possibility of Failure

From New Testament times there have been church members who have failed to exemplify in daily living those high standards of behavior which Jesus indicates for his disciples. Have they been the happy people of the churches? Far from it. Ananias and Sapphira, who practiced deception against their fellow church members, came to an early grave (Acts 5:1–11). Simon the sorcerer professed conversion, but sought to secure spiritual powers by mercenary means, and was publicly rebuked (Acts 8:9–24). Hymenaeus and Alexander betrayed the faith and their names are ignominiously mentioned as warnings to others (1 Tim. 1:20). Demas lacked in loyalty and forsook imprisoned Paul when he most needed friendship, because, as the apostle accusingly wrote, he "loved this present world" (2 Tim. 4:10). Diotrephes abused his position in the church for reasons of personal vanity, and the record of his shameful conduct may be read to this day (3 John 9).

One entire epistle (1 Corinthians) had to be written because a church had compromised with evil. In eleven chapters out of sixteen the apostle deals with the sins and shortcomings of that church membership. "Carnal" was the word he used to describe these people (1 Cor. 3:1–3). Instead of being spiritually motivated they were creatures of flesh, obeying the impulses of their bodies rather than yielding to the Spirit of God. The offenses of which they were guilty make an ugly list. But all sin is ugly in the sight of God, and never uglier than when it is committed or condoned by those who belong to the fellowship of Christ's church.

These were searching words when they were written, and they are still the supreme test of Christian behavior: "Know ye not that your body is the temple of the Holy Ghost which is in you, which ye have of God, and ye are not your own? For ye are bought with a price: therefore glorify God in your body, and in your spirit, which are God's" (1 Cor. 6:19-20).

4. *The Magnificence of Success*

Do you remember the story of Lazarus? After his resurrection we are told that great crowds gathered in his home town of Bethany, "not for Jesus' sake only, but that they might see Lazarus also, whom he had raised from the dead." The opportunity of seeing this walking miracle had an amazing result, for "many of the Jews went away, and believed on Jesus" (John 12:9, 11).

Lazarus was a witness who testified to the divine power of Jesus through his new life. Though he and his sisters lived almost under the shadow of the walls of Jerusalem and though the Jewish religious leaders had made plain their bitter enmity toward Jesus, these three people demonstrated their love and loyalty to the Master by giving a feast in his honor. That was witnessing at its brightest and best. No wonder that God took hold of this courageous testimony and used it to bring others to know Jesus as their Saviour and Lord.

The greatest argument for Christianity is a transformed life, and the greatest joy of Christianity is the privilege of witnessing for him whose grace makes the transformation. The apostle spoke for every Christian when he said: "The love of Christ constraineth us; because we thus judge, that if one died for all, then were all dead; and that he died for all, that they which live should not henceforth live unto themselves, but unto him which died for them, and rose again" (2 Cor. 5:14–15).

Are you living for Jesus, church member? Until you do, you will not know the real joy of Christian discipleship.

II. WITNESSING BY DIRECT ACTION

1. *Each One Win One*

Among the grandest words ever written are these, "And he brought him to Jesus" (John 1:42). The first addition to the circle of Christ's friends was the result of personal evangelism. Andrew went out after his brother Simon and introduced him to Jesus. Who can measure the joy of that moment, or say whose joy was the greatest—Andrew's or Simon's or Jesus' himself?

Of course, Andrew and Simon became apostles, which might suggest that only apostles ("full-time workers" we would call them today) are expected to engage in evangelism of this kind. So it is as well to refer to another gospel incident. In Gadara there lived a poor demented man who was a menace to himself and the community in which he lived. "No man could bind him, no, not with chains," reads the record (Mark 5:1–20), proceeding to tell how attempts had been made to restrain him, but all to no avail. Then Jesus came into this man's tortured world and spoke the word which delivered him from the demons that held him in their grip. In overflowing grati- tude the healed demoniac asked leave to join the com- pany of Jesus. But this was the answer he received: "Go home to thy friends, and tell them how great things the Lord hath done for thee, and hath had compassion on thee." He did that, and more, for we are told that he "began to publish in Decapolis [not one city, but ten!] how great things Jesus had done for him: and all men

did marvel." What unmistakable joy there is in those
words!

We miss God's purpose for us if we do not share the
blessing of our salvation with others. Do you know what
it is to look across the church auditorium during the worship hour and see the face of someone who is there, in
fellowship with God's people, because you witnessed to
him?

2. *Opportunities in the Church*

Our study together has emphasized the opportunities
for significant service which the Christian may find in the
program of his church. As we now think of personal witness for Jesus, we need to realize that the organizations
of the church abound in ready-made situations for soul-
winning. Undoubtedly the greatest of these is the Sunday
school class. The teacher and every saved member of the
class has a responsibility for those who are unsaved and
an unparalleled opportunity to win them to Christ.
Prayer must certainly be offered for their salvation, but
prayer must lead to action. Graciously, humbly, persua-
sively we must tell them what Jesus means to us, pleading
with them to commit their own lives into his strong
hands. The reward of such endeavor surpasses description. "They that be wise [teachers] shall shine as the
brightness of the firmament; and they that turn many
to righteousness as the stars for ever and ever" (Dan. 12:
3). That spells joy!

3. *Speak a Word for Jesus!*

Some of the greatest trophies that have been won for
Jesus Christ have not been reached by planned evangelism but by casual conversation with a keen Christian.
When in the course of life's daily contacts we use opportunities to speak a word for our Master, we can never tell

what the consequences may be. It is expected of the preacher in the pulpit that he will plead with souls to accept Christ. But when a housewife speaks to the milkman of his need of salvation, when a passenger shows interest in the spiritual welfare of the taxi driver, or when the store clerk asks her fellow employee to go to church with her, that is unexpected—and the result may be unexpected, too. For thousands of people around us are spiritually hungry, and someone may be waiting for the very word we can speak. Of course, the results of "gossiping the gospel" in this way may never be known in this life. But the joys of which we think are for eternity as well as now; and what could make heaven more heavenly than to find people there who trusted the Saviour because of something we said?

III. WITNESSING THROUGH THE CHRISTIAN HOME

1. *The Church in the House*

Of the church and the home it may be said, "What God hath joined together, let no man put asunder." In patriarchal days, the head of the family was also its priest. Long before there was a tabernacle in which to worship, each home had its altar. And long afterward we are told of Samuel that, after he had completed each circuit of duty as judge in Israel, "his return was to Ramah; for there was his house; and there he judged Israel; and there he built an altar unto the Lord" (1 Sam. 7:17). Was it not an explanation of Samuel's spiritual strength that he took his worship into his home?

When we arrive in the New Testament, we find the closest link between church and home; in fact, to begin with, Christians had no better place in which to meet than their homes. So we have the phrase, recurring in slightly varying forms, "the church in thy house"

(Philemon 2; Rom. 16:5; 1 Cor. 16:19; Col. 4:15). Until ever-increasing memberships made special meeting places necessary, it was the privilege of church members to open their homes for purposes of worship and witness.

If we are to achieve the joys of church membership at their fullest, we must conserve this God-ordained union of church and home. Since the Lord may be as much with his people in their dining rooms as he is when they join with others in the services of the church, it behooves them to see that table talk and table manners are worthy of the divine Guest. And this is true of everything that goes on within a Christian home. House room should be given to nothing that would grieve the Lord or give occasion of stumbling to any of his little ones.

The witness of a Christian home is a beautiful thing. Thanksgiving before meals and family worship at an appointed time each day should mark every church member's home. And these things testify boldly for Christ. But so also does the spirit of mutual patience, consideration, sympathy, and love which should characterize such homes. Many a careless, indifferent person has been brought near to God by visiting in a home where Christ is the acknowledged head.

2. *Carrying Sunday into Weekdays*

A significant movement, now rapidly gaining ground, relates Sunday activities in the church to weekday interests in the home. Parents who want to know what their children do in Sunday school and Training Union may have their questions answered by a special feature in *Home Life*. There the programs of Sunday morning and evening, as engaged in by Nursery, Beginner, and Primary children, are reviewed in the light of home needs; and help is offered to parents who want to strengthen the link between church and home by sharing and developing their children's Sunday interests. Those who take advantage of these facilities are proving that the joys of church membership may overflow into the domestic scene by the enrichment of family relationships on the level of spiritual activity.

3. *America's Great Need*

Great civilizations of the past have perished by reason, among other things, of the decay of family life. Where marriage vows are lightly broken, home blessings are little esteemed, and parental authority is ignored, there are the seeds of national deterioration and disaster. The remedy for all such tendencies is the gospel of Jesus Christ; and the glorious alternative is the multiplication of homes in which Christ is honored, God's Word is read, family worship is observed, and the family is linked by indissoluble bonds with the fellowship of the church.

There are three great institutions which have the blessing of almighty God: civil government, church, and home. True happiness, experienced on the widest scale, depends upon loyalty to all three. When the compass of life finds its center in the church, then the circle which it strikes will be large enough to contain all other worthy loyalties, and these will be bound together by the unbreakable ties of love for God and for our fellows.

IV. WITNESSING BY LOYAL CHURCH MEMBERSHIP

1. *An Example to Follow*

Early in this study we saw how the conditions which prevailed in the first church fellowship created a testimony which resulted in the salvation of others: "And the Lord added to the church daily such as should be saved" (Acts 2:47). This was a happy church, harmonious in its inner relationships, industrious in its activities, aggressive in its witness to the truths of the gospel. God used that church, as he continues to use churches today which pattern themselves on this apostolic example.

Baptists believe that, in doctrine and practice, their churches conform to the apostolic order. But it is necessary to remember that the risen and glorified Lord addressed these words to one church: "I know thy works, that thou hast a name that thou livest, and art dead" (Rev. 3:1). A name is not enough, whether it be a New Testament name or a Baptist name. A church is more than doctrine and ordinances and program. A church is *people,* and its real values are not to be found in the style of its buildings or the decorum of its services or the magnificence of its preaching or even in the size of its budget. The real values of a church, whereby its effectiveness in the service of Christ is determined, exist in the character of its members.

2. *A Saviour to Serve*

We have discussed the joys of church membership—a worthy and proper theme. But there is a joy more important than the joy of any church member or of any church. That is the joy of Jesus Christ himself. If we make our own satisfaction the aim of our church activity, we shall unquestionably fail. If we make his joy the object of our lives, then in bringing gladness to his heart we shall bring certain blessing to ourselves.

Is it not important to remember that the joy which Jesus eventually attained was reached along a road of self-denial and suffering? "Let us run with patience the race that is set before us," wrote the author of Hebrews, "looking unto Jesus the author and finisher of our faith; who for the joy that was set before him endured the cross, despising the shame, and is set down at the right hand of the throne of God" (Heb. 12:1–2). The joys of church membership are not of the carnival kind: not passing thrills but lasting satisfactions, realized sometimes after much toil and many tears. But they are joys which have no equal and which none can take away. For they belong to eternity and not to time; they are the gift of God to his faithful people.

3. *A Covenant to Keep*

The psalmist said of God's precepts, "In keeping of them there is great reward" (Psalm 19:11). He had proved the blessings of obedience. Having pledged himself to the observance of the divine law, he made the happy discovery that life became richer and fuller in proportion as he made God's will the determining factor in all of his actions.

The church member has also made a vow to God. It is expressed for him in his church covenant. The terms of that covenant invite our constant thoughtful consideration, for of them also it may be said, "In keeping of them there is great reward."

As a concluding exercise for this study, it is suggested that the class stand and repeat together either the words of their own church covenant or the following statement which is used in many Southern Baptist churches:

"Having been led, as we believe, by the Spirit of God to receive the Lord Jesus Christ as our Saviour; and, on the profession of our faith, having been baptized in the name of the Father, and of the Son, and of the Holy Ghost, we do now, in the presence of God, angels, and this assembly, most solemnly and joyfully enter into covenant with one another, as one body in Christ.

"We engage, therefore, by the aid of the Holy Spirit, to walk together in Christian love; to strive for the advancement of this church, in knowledge, holiness, and comfort; to promote its prosperity and spirituality; to sustain its worship, ordinances, discipline, and doctrines; to contribute cheerfully and regularly to the support of the ministry, the expenses of the church, the relief of the poor, and the spread of the gospel through all nations.

"We also engage to maintain family and secret devotion; to religiously educate our children; to seek the salvation of our kindred and acquaintances; to walk circumspectly in the world; to be just in our dealings, faithful in our engagements, and exemplary in our deportment; to avoid all tattling, backbiting, and excessive anger; to abstain from the sale and use of intoxicating drinks as a beverage; and to be zealous in our efforts to advance the kingdom of our Saviour.

"We further engage to watch over one another in brotherly love; to remember each other in prayer; to aid each other in sickness and distress; to cultivate Christian sympathy in feeling and courtesy in speech; to be slow to take offense, but always ready for reconciliation, and, mindful of the rules of our Saviour, to secure it without delay.

"We moreover engage, that when we remove from this place, we will as soon as possible unite with some other church, where we can carry out the spirit of this covenant and the principles of God's Word."

SUGGESTED TOPICS FOR DISCUSSION

1. Name some New Testament characters who (1) failed to live up to their profession of faith, and (2) who bore a good witness.

2. What opportunities for soul-winning does your church program afford?

3. Discuss ways by which Christian homes may witness for the Lord.

OUTLINE

I. WITNESSING BY PERSONAL LIFE

1. By Our Experience of Salvation
2. By the Proof of Regeneration
3. The Possibility of Failure
4. The Magnificence of Success

II. WITNESSING BY DIRECT ACTION

1. Each One Win One
2. Opportunities in the Church
3. Speak a Word for Jesus!

III. WITNESSING THROUGH THE CHRISTIAN HOME

1. The Church in the House
2. Carrying Sunday into Weekdays
3. America's Greatest Need

IV. WITNESSING BY LOYAL CHURCH MEMBERSHIP

1. An Example to Follow
2. A Saviour to Serve
3. A Covenant to Keep

QUESTIONS FOR REVIEW AND EXAMINATION

FOR INSTRUCTIONS concerning the examination and the requesting of awards, see Directions for the Teaching and the Study of This Book for Credit, page 135.

Chapter 1

1. What marks of a Christian are given in this chapter?
2. Give some reasons why a Christian should also be a church member.
3. Compile a list under the heading: "Ways not to enjoy being a church member."

Chapter 2

4. Are rules of membership customary to organizations? Give examples.
5. Outline briefly the first occasions recorded in the New Testament when additions were made to a church.
6. What are the essential qualifications for church membership?
7. Is the New Testament method of baptism important? Substantiate your answer from the Scriptures.

Chapter 3

8. On what grounds is Jesus described as Lord of the church?
9. Give reasons for rejecting the idea of Pentecost as "the birthday of the church."
10. What contrasted methods did Satan employ to silence the witness of the church?
11. What addition to the American Constitution signalizes the success of Baptist witness to the separation of church and state?

Chapter 4

12. What is implied by the statement that there is a "God-shaped vacuum" in the human heart?
13. What is meant by "revealed religion"?
14. What is "the supreme stimulus of worship"?
15. What differences has Calvary made to the practices of worship?

Chapter 5

16. What common experience furnishes the basis for fellowship in the church?

17. How may we enjoy "fellowship in learning" in our church life today?
18. Describe some opportunities for social fellowship which your church provides.
19. Comment upon the statement: "The program of Southern Baptists has the Christian family as its ideal and objective."

Chapter 6

20. Quote Bible passages to show that the church has always been at the heart of God's redemptive plan.
21. Learn and write down the membership statistics for your church—total, resident, nonresident, active, and inactive.
22. How may the church member serve his community?
23. Discuss the possibilities of personal development through Christian service.

Chapter 7

24. Where should our Christian service begin? Give biblical support for your answer.
25. What should be the minimum standard of Christian giving? Mention a worthy incentive to such giving.
26. Name the agencies of the Southern Baptist Convention, its commissions, and its standing committees.
27. How was the Baptist World Alliance inaugurated? What do you know of the last Baptist World Congress?

Chapter 8

28. Upon what foundation must we build a Christian character?
29. What reminder has God given of the necessity for the Christian to "walk in newness of life"?
30. Give scriptural support for the statement that every saved person should witness for Jesus.
31. Whose joy should be the first aim and ambition of every church member?

DIRECTIONS FOR THE TEACHING AND THE STUDY OF THIS BOOK FOR CREDIT

I. DIRECTIONS FOR THE TEACHER

1. Ten class periods of forty-five minutes each, or the equivalent, are required for the completion of this book for credit.

2. The teacher of the class is given an award on the book if he requests it.

3. The teacher shall give a written examination covering the subject matter in the textbook, and the student shall make a minimum grade of 70 per cent. The examination may take the form of assigned work to be done between the class sessions, or as a final examination at the end of the course.

EXCEPTION: All who attend all of the class sessions; who read the book through by the close of the course; and who, in the judgment of the teacher, do the classwork satisfactorily may be exempted from taking the examination.

4. In the Graded Training Union Study Course, a seal for Subject 2, The Church, is granted to adults for the completion of this book.

Sunday school credit may be elected by the pupil. Application for Sunday school awards should be sent to the state Sunday school department and for Training Union awards to the state Training Union department. These departments will provide the forms for these applications. They should be made in duplicate and both copies sent.

II. DIRECTIONS FOR THE STUDENT

1. *In Classwork*

(1) The pupil must attend at least six of the ten forty-five minute class periods to be entitled to take the class examination.

(2) The pupil must certify that the textbook has been

read. (In rare cases where pupils may find it impracticable to
read the book before the completion of the classwork, the
teacher may accept a promise to read the book carefully
within the next two weeks.)

(3) The pupil must take a written examination, making
a minimum grade of 70 per cent. (All who attend all of the
class sessions; who read the book through by the close of the
course; and who, in the judgment of the teacher, do satis-
factory classwork may be exempted from taking the examination.)

2. *In Individual Study by Correspondence*

Those who for any reason wish to study the book without
the guidance of a teacher will use one of the following
methods:

(1) Write answers to the questions printed in the book, or

(2) Write a development of the chapter outlines.

If the second method is used, the student will study the
book and then with the open book write a development of
the chapter outlines.

In either case the student must read the book through.

Students may find profit in studying the text together, but
where awards are requested, individual papers are required.
Carbon copies or duplicates in any form cannot be accepted.

All written work done by such students on books for Sunday school credit should be sent to the state Sunday school
secretary. All of such work done on books for Training Union
credit should be sent to the state Training Union secretary.

III. INTERCHANGE OF CREDITS AND AWARDS ON COMPARABLE SUBJECTS

One award, either for Training Union or Sunday school, is
granted for completing this book.

J. E. LAMBDIN
Secretary, Training Union Department
Baptist Sunday School Board

C. AUBREY HEARN
Director of the Study Course